THE LEGEND OF

PORT ELLEN

DISTILLERY

Röse 21 D-31832 Springe
www.unibuchverlag.de

Druck: gutenberg beuys freindruckerei gmbh, Langenhagen

ISBN: 978-3-934900-63-9

Bibliografische Information der Deutschen Nationalbibliothek
Die Deutsche Nationalbibliothek verzeichnet diese Publikation in der Deutschen Nationalbibliografie; detaillierte bibliografische Daten sind über http://dnb.d-nb.de abrufbar.

The Legend of Port Ellen Distillery

PREFACE

This book is an endeavour to document the history of the famous and beloved Port Ellen Distillery.

The name Port Ellen will always be closely tied to the name of the successful entrepreneur and later owner John Ramsay. Ramsay played an important role in both the utilization of distillery technology as well as marketing Scottish whisky, particularly by exporting it to the United States.

In the summer of 1996, I acquired my first bottle of Port Ellen on Islay. This has since triggered a passion to collect Port Ellen bottlings as well as information about the distillery, which by then had already been shut down for 13 years. Due to having graduated in history, I started to focus my historical interest on this particular distillery. My passion for whisky and the acquaintance with Ludwig and Bärbel Reifferscheid (owner of a well known whisky business), that over the years has developed into a friendship, have opened avenues to many well-known personalities in the sphere of whisky both at home and abroad. From the numerous contacts that I have had, I would particularly like to highlight those with Professor Walther Schobert, Grant Carmichael and the brothers Fred and Stewart Laing.

During the research for this book, which had been further intensified after the turn of the millennium, I received invaluable encouragement and support from many friends and other persons. However there were also, drawbacks as sources that could have promoted my research were constantly referring to their company secret and thus not accesible. 32 years after the final shut down of the distillery, this research now sometimes resembles a 1.000 piece jigsaw puzzle with many pieces of it missing.

Therefore, certain issues in this book will remain speculative while others are probably never going to be solved.
It is my hope that I was successful in compiling all the information about Port Ellen which previously had been spread across various works, in one single edition for the first time.

This book is aimed at preserving the legacy of Port Ellen Distillery beyond the day, when the last Port Ellen casks will be bottled, which is likely to come during the next decade.

Port Ellen,
one of the twin pagodes, 2014

FUJIFILM DOF
1906
539B
RR&C°
B

Port Ellen, workforce 1906

Port Ellen Distillery in 1920

To encourage the legal distillation of whisky, the Excise Act of 1823 introduced a reduction of the duty on spirits from a rather exorbitant to a more moderate level. It also brought the compulsory introduction of the spirit safe in distilleries, but not before tests had been made to ensure that it had no harmful effects on the quality of the product. The official experiments were carried out by Mister Fox at Port Ellen during the winter of 1823/24. Therefore Port Ellen seems to be the first distillery that had a spirit safe installed. It was later improved by John Ramsay (1814-1892) and James Stein from Ardenistiel Distillery. (1)
The Port Ellen Distillery had been developed from a malt mill by Alexander Kerr MacKay and started its production in 1825. The first manager was John Morrison from Alloa, a cousin of the later distillery owner, John Ramsay. Things did not go well at Port Ellen under John Morrison's management. From 10th October 1826 to 10th October 1827 the total production was 3,179 gallons of proof spirit. (The House of Commons 19 July 1828)
During this time, the Ramsay family and their relatives had a family interest in this Islay-distillery. Therefore, the Procurator Fiscal of Clackmannan, Ebenezer Ramsay, who was in charge of the extensive distilling interests around Alloa, ordered his son, Eben Ramsay, to deliver a report on the problems with the new distillery. Being non-compliant with the request, Eben subsequently sent his nephew John Ramsay to Islay in 1832 to find out about these problems. (2)
John Ramsay, the youngest son in a family of seven, was born on August 15, 1814 into a family of farmers, businessmen and tradesmen. John and his two brothers were educated in Stirling under the famous dominie, Peter MacDougall. When he was twelve years old John left home seeking for fortune. At the age of 13 he was working as a cotton mill clerk. He payed for his own education (taking Latin lessons and repaying reading debts on library subscriptions). Ramsay had many talents, especially his business acumen. (3)
When he was casting for a better job, he considered offers for employment in both South Africa (Natal) and India. Because of the

Ramsay family he went to analyse the Port Ellen business. He was soon convinced that the Port Ellen Distillery could be made profitable and wrote his uncle accordingly.
When his eldest brother, Thomas Ramsay, who had worked as a shipbuilder in Miramachi, in New Brunswick, Canada came to assist him, it was finally agreed that John Ramsay should go to Alloa to be taught in the art of di-

stilling by James Morrison, a brother of John Morrison. After having finished this training, he was manager of he Port Ellen Distillery for an annual salary of £150. His cousin John Morrison was assigned the task to sell the whisky in Glasgow, while his brother Thomas would be responsible for purchasing the necessary grain.
The arrangement, however, proved to be unsuccessful from the start. Thomas Ramsay soon realised that John Morrison proved to be impossible to work with as a partner; he therefore quit the job and returned home to Canada. The second son of Ebenezer Ramsay, another Thomas Ramsay, now became a new partner, and John Morrison was finally removed from the partnership. Later on John Morrison was installed in Ardenistiel Distillery, Islay, only to fail again. He finally returned to Glasgow as an embittered man. The Glasgow agency was given to Mr. J. Richardson, who held it for many years. (4)
In 1833, Major James Adair of Dunfries and Glasgow who held the lease for the Port Ellen buildings, purchased the remaining years of the ground lease. He had made friends with John Ramsay and allowed him free reign to establish his business. Although barely in his twenties, John Ramsay had already earned a good reputation with the many businessmen he was dealing with in Glasgow and Islay.

Under Ramsay's management the distillery gradually expanded and a second duty-free warehouse was added in 1839, due to the increase in business. Ramsay however remained however, only a tenant. After Adair died in 1840, the leases became vacant and the distillery was put up for sale. If he were to consolidate his business interests in Port Ellen, John Ramsay badly needed the leases. However, legally the distillery and the leases were up for auction to the highest bidder. Walter Frederick Campbell, whose ancestor Daniel Campbell of Shawfield had bought Islay and a part of Jura for £12,000 in the early 18th century, exercised his right of pre-emption upon expiry of the leases and assured that his partner Ramsay was able to purchase the distillery for £1,950 and a new lease. (5)
In 1840, at the age of 25, Ramsay had gained control over the first of the four Kildalton Distilleries. Once he had repaid Campbell, he took out leases on two neighbouring farms at Cornabus and Kilnaughton, finally settling in Port Ellen as farmer and distiller. He profited from the widespread family business and did not hesitate to start exporting large proportion of the Port Ellen output to North America.
He also imported sherry and Madeira wine and realised that the casks of these wines were having a beneficial effect on the maturing and colouring of whisky.
Besides the success that was showing in his business affairs, John Ramsay had also inherited money from the Ramsay uncles and aunts that had passed away over the years.
By 1842, his Port Ellen Distillery inventory showed 7,399 gallons (33,590 litres) of whisky in bond, worth £1,479 16s out of a whole stock in bond, including barley, beer, peats, coals, and feints amounting to £4,193 19s 8d. (6)
Being chosen to test the spirit safe at Port Ellen that finally led to the improvement of this device, Ramsay also tested a patent still. For

three years the distillery worked a Stein patent still with malt only. (7)
In a letter from Walter Campbell to John Ramsay, dated 8th April, 1844, the depth of their relationship becomes apparent. Not only does Campbell reveal his serious health problems to Ramsay in this letter, he also urges him to take advantage of the fact that Queen Victoria was purchasing Port Ellen Whisky for Her Majesty's cellar in order to generate a greater demand for the product.
In 1848 in his capacity as distillers spokesman, he actively sought to have restrictions lifted that barred spirits from being exported in capacities exceeding 80 gallons as well as negating the right to store whisky in bond, duty free, for export. Not only were the Port Ellen warehouses some of the earliest to be constructed for this purpose, they also had a reputation for beeing amongst the best.
By this time, his sister Margaret had joined him at Cornabus farm and got married to James Stein, who had been managing Ardenistiel Distillery together with his brother Andrew. Stein became Ramsay's factor and distillery manager and effectively freed him so that he was able to attend to his affairs in Glasgow, where he imported sherry and Madeira wine, and coincidentally had a house in Madeira Court.
Walter Frederick Campbell had encouraged John Ramsay to buy a steamer for the purpose of running a cargo service between the islands and Glasgow. This was the 'Modern Athens' and from that point on he owned a ship, or had an interest in several other boats and also became active in the clipper trade with the East Indies (the 'Ramsay Edda')
Walter Frederick Campbell of Shawfield himself was not a man of business. Even for John Ramsay it was impossible to save the heavily indebted Campbell estate. On 2nd December 1847 Campbell finally agreed to sequestration, when the rental arrears owed to his estate stood at £32,095. Personal debt, heritable bonds and bank loans accounted to over £750,000 and the income from his estates was insufficient to pay even the interest on his loans.
In the end, Campbell's debts reached £815,000 or about £46,1 millions in 1998 equivalence. (8)
His estates were put up for sale in November 1848 with an asking price of £540,000 for his land on Islay.
As no prospective buyer came forth with an offer, his son John Francis Campbell and John Ramsay held the whole estate in trust until August 1853. During this period, the creditors were represented by James Brown, an Edinburgh accountant.
In August 1853, when James Morrison acquired the Islay estate at the reduced price of £451,000, Ramsay had cannily negotiated the future purchase of the Kildalton portion for the sum of £82,265. In 1855, he became owner and landlord of the Laphroaig, Ardenistiel, Lagavulin and Ardbeg Distilleries with all the associated farms, pastures and distillery villages. Ramsay assured that the Kildalton Distillery leaseholders enjoyed long leases and had properly secured water rights, something that was frequently overlooked in those days. (9)

By this time, Ramsay withdrew from this northern trade and persuaded Charles Morrison, the eldest son of James of Basildon, to become half-owner of the 'Islay', a steamer purchased by Walter Frederick Campbell for the benefit of the island, in which several distillers had a share, John Ramsay's being the largest. He then concentrated on a bi-weekly cargo and passenger service between Islay and Glasgow, including calls at Port Rush in Northern Ireland and West Loch Tarbert on the Argyll mainland.

1865 and 1866 saw the peak of an economic boom that had hit Great Britain some years before and subsequently the output of malt- and grain whisky increased. Pot still malt whisky production from 1864 to 1866 was about 5,000.000 gallons compared to 3,500.000 gallons in 1861. (10)

The increase in output was accompanied by major rebuilding of the distilleries. Port Ellen, Rosebank, Falkirk, Banff and Ben Nevis distilleries all underwent reconstruction between 1863 and 1865.

In the 1860s, Port Ellen Distillery filled over ten washbacks a week. The output was 115.000 gallons (550.000 litres) of spirit a year. (11)

By 1861, John Ramsay had added the rest of the overpopulated Oa peninsula and other holdings as Laggan and Island to his lands for another £45,000. He clearly recognised the main problem of too many tenants on the land, particularly on Oa. (12)

Being concerned about the poverty, overcrowding and even famine on the Islay farms, Ramsay assisted many families to emigrate, knowing that they might stand a better chance to improve their lives overseas. What could be interpreted as an act of philanthropy was however interpreted by some critics as „Enforced removals", in the same vein as the clearances, and Ramsay faced a barrage of criticism from the press and in the House of Commons. To satisfy his own concerns, and those of his critics, he travelled to Canada on his own in 1870 to see at first-hand how his former tenants were faring.

Ramsay even became a Member of the Parliament himself. He was MP for Stirling burghs in 1868, and for the Falkirk Burghs from 1874 to 1880, and again from 1880 to 1885. Following the general election in February 1874, Ramsay was disqualified from sitting in Parliament because he was holding a Government contract. Therefore, Ramsay transferred the ownership of the boat 'Islay' to Charles Morrison, though he continued its management. Ramsay won the following by-election held on 26 March 1874 and again returned as MP for Stirling Burghs.

In 1878, the boat was sold to David Hutcheson, who pioneered the daily steamship services to the Western Isles. Hutcheson was succeeded by his young partner, David MacBrayne, whose name is now almost synonymous with the west of Scotland .

John Ramsay had also taken a great interest in education, a fact reflected by his provision of schools and schooling on Islay. (13)

The Glasgow end of the business had been managed by James Richardson, followed by William Phaup Lowrie (1831-1916), who left in 1869 to start up his own business, successfully blending and bottling Scotch whisky in bond. Although he was later erroneously

credited for having initiated these practices in Scotland, he has introduced some innovations into the production and marketing of Scotch remaining with us until today. Lowrie was the first to pre-treat casks when a shortage of sherry butts for fillings occurred during the late 19th century, and he installed a large bottling plant at his works in Washington Street, Glasgow that effectively made his operation self-contained.
As one of the early blenders, Lowrie became one of the leaders of the trade in the 1880s and 1890s. The connections between John Ramsay and his former employee were close. Port Ellen Whisky at this time was a highly flavoured malt suitable for blending. (14)
In 1885, the famous distilling historian Alfred Barnard started his work for Haper's Weekly Gazette. As a secretary for his new employer, he came to see every working whisky distillery in Great Britain and Ireland from 1885-1886. In all, he visited 162 distilleries; 129 in Scotland, 29 in Ireland and 4 in England, resulting in the monumental 500-page-book 'The Whisky Distilleries of the United Kingdom', covering in depth technical information on the distilleries along with sketches and engravings.

During his visit on Islay in 1886, he inspected the Port Ellen Distillery too. Barnard wrote:
"Proprietor: James Ramsay.
Before visiting the Distillery, which is the subject of this brief chapter, we took a stroll along the shore to get a breath of the sea. Port Ellen possesses most delightful bathing sands, which would if cottages were available, and the place were nearer Glasgow. The lighthouse, at the opposite end of the bay from the Distillery, was erected in 1832, by the late Mr. W. F. Campbell of Islay, to the memory of his wife, Lady Ellinor, and is a conspicuous object from any part of the coast.
The Port Ellen Distillery is planted on the seashore, about half a mile from the village. The works cover three acres, and were built in the year 1825, but since that time several important additions have been made. In the absence of the manager, to whom we had letters of introduction, the distiller conducted us over the premises. We were first taken to the three spacious Barley Lofts, well lighted and ventilated, of the following dimensions, No. 1 is 100 feet long and 36 wide; No. 2, 110 feet by 52; No. 3, 135 feet by 30. The three Malting Floors are of the same size, each having the usual Steeps; in close proximity are two Kilns, floored with wire cloth, one 52 feet by 26, the other 36 feet square. A flight of steps leads into the Malt Store, off which is the Mill Room, containing a pair of malt rollers; and in the adjoining room is the Mash Tun, 14 feet in diameter by 5 feet deep, a Wash Charger containing 5,000 gallons, two heating tanks, etc.

From this department we proceeded to the Tun Room, which contains seven Fermenting-backs, of an average capacity of 7,000 gallons each. Passing from here we came to the Still House, containing two old Pot Stills, one holding 3,500 gallons and the other 2,100, also two Receivers, holding 1,400 and 1,600 gallons respectively. In a line with the Distillery are six handsome Warehouses, containing at the time of our visit 3,700 casks, holding 240,000 gallons of Whisky of different ages. We may here remark that only peat which is dug in the district is used in the drying, and the water comes from two lochs in the hills; the principal one used for distilling purposes is noted in the locality for its clearness and purity,

the other is used for driving purposes. Elevators are used all over the works; there is a Cooperage and Seasoning House for casks, a fine Spirit Store, and one of Morton's Refrigerators. The Whisky is Islay Malt, and the annual output 140,000 gallons." (15)

Barnard seems to be somewhat disappointed that the Port Ellen manager has had no time for him during his visit. He did, however, provide good information about the distillery premises, the distillery equipment and the annual output.

Despite the fact that Barnard classifies the two pot stills as old, the works at Port Ellen were more up to date and mechanised than those at Lagavulin and Laphroaig. Lagavulin was producing 75,000 gallons a year while Laphroaig was turning out 23,000 gallons. (16)

Since the 1860s Port Ellen's output had incre-

ased by 25,000 gallons of spirit a year.
Three years before his death in 1892, John Ramsay granted a lease to his second wife Lucy for the land on the seaward side of the distillery. Here she built four villas - one for herself (in the event of her daughter getting married) and the others for distillery and excise workers. Her involvement in the distillery deepened when Ramsay died at Kildalton House on January 24th, 1892, aged 77; and the day-to-day running of the business passed over to her.
John Ramsay was certainly the most influential figure on Islay in the nineteenth century.

In September 1892, a special meeting was convened to determine ,payments to Mrs. Ramsay for spirits at Port Ellen, sold during John Ramsay's lifetime but not delivered, which stood at 160,287 gallons (727,700 litres) by the end of June, 1892.
The valuators were A.W. Robertson of Robertson and Baxter, the Glasgow whisky brokers, and the former Port Ellen employee W.P. Lowie. Between them they fixed the price of the peats, feints, malt and coals taken over by Mrs Ramsay as follows:
1,200 carts of peats at 2s a cart.
359 gallons feints at 1s per proof gallon.
400 bushels of Malt at 25s a quarter.
25 tons coals at 10s a ton.
Lucy Ramsay, an eminently practical woman, took over the control of the distillery with the help of a new manager, Mr. Osborne. She had never favoured John Ramsay's grandnephew and manager, J R Stein. Stein would leave the firm no later than 30th September 1892 with a final pay cheque of £16 13s 4d. (17)

Lucy Ramsay died in 1905. Her son Iain Ramsay, then aged 27, took over the business while his mother's capital in the plant was inherited by his sister, Miss Lucy Ramsay. From this point on, Iain Ramsay struggled the best he could to keep the distillery business on a sound footing.

In 1909 the Chancellor of the Exchequer Lloyd George raised the duty on spirits to the level of 15 shillings per proof gallon. In the ensuing 11 years the excise duty on spirits was raised sixfold. (18)

Ian Ramsay was forced to find a business partner in 1912, when his sister decided to lift her capital from the business to buy an estate on the mainland. During that time, he was employing Malcolm Macintyre of Train & Macintyre Limited as a trainee distiller and agreed to take him in just as the First World War was looming over Europe.

Ramsay and his partner Macintyre both served during the war as soldiers but only Ramsay survived. Discharged with the rank of captain and war-disabled he returned, only to find out that his stored household effects had all been destroyed in a Zeppelin raid on Glasgow. (19)

Port Ellen workforce 1895

Port Ellen workforce 1906

His business was in want of capital and his whisky markets had rapidly receded due to the effects of the war and the prohibition in the United States. The latter hit the Port Ellen business hard because the distillery lost its most important export market for which it had provided whisky over more than half a century.
His battlefield injuries left Ramsay was in bad state of health too The constant lack of money pressed him to sell his father's distilleries one after the other.

In 1920, James Buchanan & Company Limited acquired Port Ellen Distillery and its assets in partnership with John Dewar & Sons Limited and formed the Port Ellen Distillery Company Limited. W.P. Lowrie's vast knowledge of Port Ellen Distillery may have moved Buchanan to acquire the distillery. For years Lowrie had acted as Buchanan's main supplier and since his retirement in 1906, his firm was owned by James Buchanan. (20)

At the beginning of the 20th century the whisky industry was in turmoil. Companies were crashing, mergers and acquisitions were rife and the giant Distillers Company Ltd. (DCL) had been formed. To protect themselves against a hostile takeover, Buchanan and Dewar founded the Scotch Whisky Brands Ltd. in 1915. This company was renamed Buchanan-Dewar Ltd. in 1919 and by 1922 it had acquired interests in eleven distilleries. Despite the prohibition in the United States, which put a damper on sales the company continued to grow and bought a total of six distilleries between 1919 and 1923 to supply whisky for its blends, including facilities in Ord, Parkmore, Port Ellen, Pulteney, and Aultmore.

Like his father Ian Ramsay proveded himself to be a fair partner for the other Kildalton distilleries. After the sale of Port Ellen he also sold the distilleries Lagavulin, Laphroaig and Ardbeg to the people who had leased them before. He ignored higher offers from others.
Lagavulin distillery, the farm, 100 acres of peat land and the water rights were sold after longer negotiations in the 1920s for £16,000. (21)

Ardbeg was the third of his Kildalton distilleries that Ramsay was forced to let go. Collin Hay and the Buchannan family pursued their acquisition. Ramsays accountant Robert MacFarlan from Glasgow negotiated throughout 1920 and 1921. Ardbeg was eventually sold by Ramsay in 1922. The distillery and its land changed owner for £19,000. The sale was cut into parts and finally written off by 1932. (22)

The negotiations about the price of Laphroaig took up some more time By 1924, Ian Hunter had purchased the distillery, Texa Island and Ardenstiel House. Especially in this case Ramsay ignored a higher offer by Peter Mackie (Lagavulin), who had had many quarrels with his Laphroaig neighbours since 1907. (23)
After the sale of his distilleries and parts of his estates Ramsay became a noted ornithologist and expert on the birds of Islay. He died in 1959.

Port Ellen
Distillery from sea in 1920

The attempts of the market leader Distillery Company Ltd. (DCL) to acquire its competitor Buchannan-Dewar and Johnnie Walker were successful in 1925. The takeover/merger of these companies was supported by Price Waterhouse & Co. since 1909, but was discontinued because of the First World War. After the merger of Buchanan-Dewar with DCL in 1925, Port Ellen was absorbed into the group. The Port Ellen Distillery Company Limited was voluntarily liquidated two years later as part of the DCLs rationalisation programme - largely due to the effects of the Great Depression. The assets were then acquired by John Dewar & Son Limited and W.P. Lowrie & Company Limited before being finally transferred to DCL subsidiary Scottish Malt Distillers (SMD) in 1930. (24) At this time the DCL and its subsidiaries were taking over the largest and finest stocks of maturing whisky throughout Scotland, and although Port Ellen was officially closed in 1930 , there can be no doubt that the distillery possessed an extensive stock in bond. At that time there was enough whisky warehoused in Port Ellen to last for 40 years, and the more cynical observers realise that it took entire 37 years before the distillery came on stream again. (25)

The DCL subsidiary SMD continued to operate the maltings and bonded warehouses during the closure. The maltings produced malt especially for Lagavulin distillery and the Port Ellen casks in the warehouses were used over the decades in the group's blends. Free space was used for the storage of Malt-Mill and Lagavulin casks. (26)

The rest of the distilling equipment was removed and used by other distilleries of the group.

Port Ellen
Distillery in 1935

The rebuilding of the distillery
During the 1960s the demand for Islay whisky which went into the blends of White Horse, J&B and Black & White, and that were distributed by DCL, notably increased. These Islay whiskies accounted for approximately 2 per cent of the blends. Owing inter alia to this rise in demand, it was decided to reactivate the Port Ellen Distillery by enlarging its capacities and partially rebuilding it from scratch.
The re-equipment of the Port Ellen Distillery started in the spring of 1966 and was completed on 1 April, 1967.

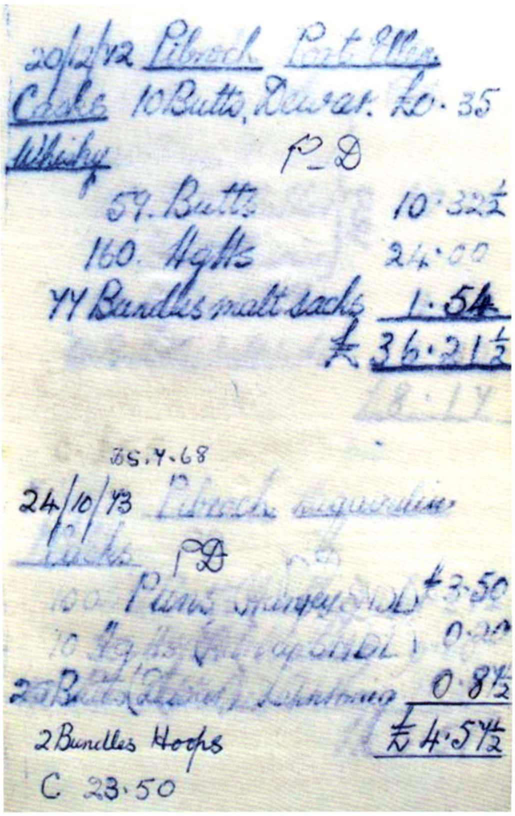

20/12/72 Pibroch Port Ellen
Casks 10 Butts, Dewar. £0·35
Whisky P.D
57. Butts 10·32½
160. Hgds 24·00
44 Bundles malt sacks 1·54
£36·21½

35.4.68
24/10/73 Pibroch
Casks PD
£3·50
0·8½
2 Bundles Hoops £4·5½
C 23·50

Port Ellen`s First Cask–April 1967
Angus Mac Taggart, Duncan Ramsay, George Ballingall

In 1966, the Eilean Sea Services began to operate a 35-ton landing craft, the 'Isle of Gigha' between Port Ellen and the mainland. Her first main contract was to bring in construction materials and equipment for rebuilding the distillery. (27)

The old distillery had been well designed, so the shells of some of the original buildings were retained. Some of the new buildings replaced others where the same part of the process had been carried out one hundred years earlier. (28)

The barley intake and dressing plant were completely renewed and upgraded. The No. 1 malt barn was unaltered but the No. 2 barn was extensively modernized by introducing a cylindro-conical steeping vessel equipped with automatic aeration. The No 2 kiln was reconstructed and a new wedge wire floor installed.

The malt storage silos were refurbished and enlarged, and a new roof was fitted. The mill room was rebuilt and a new 4-roll Porteus mill purchased. In 1932, when the distillery was temporarily shut down, the original Port Ellen mill had been transferred to the active SMD Rosebank Distillery. (29)
The process water and the cooling water were drawn from one of the nearby Leorin Lochs, where the distillery had water rights.
Port Ellen Distillery used mainly the Golden Promise and Triumph barley varieties at the end of its era. Much of the barley used in the old days was locally cultivated. Since the installation of the drum malting facility the barley has mainly been brought in from the mainland.(30)

A new mash tun of a traditional cast-iron type with a copper top was installed with the mashing process controlled from a central panel incorporating all the necessary instruments and electrical gear. It had a capacity of about five metric tonnes. At full production ten mashes were made per week. (31.)
Wort was transferred to the washbacks via an overhead filling line to prevent residual liquid in the pipe causing bacterial spoilage of the fermentation.
The tunroom roof was renewed and heightened to hold eight washbacks made of larch, each with its own electrically driven „switcher“ unit to prevent froth overflow. The washbacks had a content of 30,000 litres each.

Port Ellen First Cask

Port Ellen Distillery in the 1960s

Port Ellen **stills leaving the Aloa factory**

Port Ellen stills are installed on site

Port Ellen stillhouse

The copper distilling plant was made by R. G. Abercrombie and comprised four plain-headed stills, each feeding a copper shell and tube condenser. The capacity of the two wash stills was 28,700 litres each and that of the two spirit stills 27,500 litres each. (32)

Initially, the stills were heated by direct coal fires fed by Prior underfeed stokers and were fitted with temperature and fill height sensors to assist the stillman.

The steam raising boiler was capable of evaporating 8,000 lbs of water per hour and was fed by two Prior underfeed stokers. A new receiver room was built of steel and brick to hold two cast iron low wines and feints charging vessels.

The low wines and feints receiver was also constructed of cast iron, but the spirit receiver was made from oak staves. The spirit store walls were heightened and a new roof fitted so that an oak spirit receiver and warehouse vat with a capacity of 5,550 gallons could be installed.

This vat, along with the spirit receiver and the eight washbacks was supplied by a certain W.P. Lowrie and Company Ltd (the company set up by the Glasgow office employee of the 1860s that also owned the Port Ellen Distillery for a short period in the early 1920s).

The cost of renovating the distillery ran to around £400,000 and the main contractor was W.H. Rankine Ltd. (33)

In 2007, general manager Grant Carmichael recalled: "It was a very modern distillery, very well designed. The water came down from the Leorin Lochs – there was a pipe to the reservoir behind the distillery. The cooling water came from there, too. We had a sea-water cooling system, but it never really worked properly. Beautiful washbacks and lovely shaped stills – quite tall for Islay, though not as tall and narrow-necked as Caol Ila." (34)

Angus MacTaggert became the first manager of the refurbished distillery. The DCL was the largest distillery owner and employer on the island. They had a resident distillery inspector on Islay, who also visited the warehousing complex at the long defunct Hazelburn Distillery at Cambpeltown.

Rather than build new warehousing on Islay, DCL shipped surplus spirit from its Islay plants to Hazelburn, where it could mature in maritime conditions very similar to those on Islay, thus maintaining consistency. (35)

There is a note of the DCL production committee from 3 April 1967: „It was reported that Port Ellen Distillery had commenced operations on 2 April but would be restricted to four mashes for the first week. It was hoped that full production would be possible within three weeks". (36)

During their ownership the Scotch Malt Distillers (SMD) had introduced a number of improvements, including changing the coal-fired stills to direct oil-fired stills. In 1966, Benromach was one of the first distilleries to adopt this. Experience with these improvements was showing good results and thereafter many other SMD distilleries changed to direct oil firing. (For example Lagavulin in 1969 and Dallas Dhu in 1971)

In 1970, the Port Ellen stills were converted to steam heating via a John Thompson Multipac oil-fired boiler and the existing boiler was also replaced with a similar oil-fired one.
There is another note of the DCL production committee from 4 May 1970: "Port Ellen Distillery, which had been closed since 28th February 1970 for conversion to steam distillation, had resumes mashing on 29th April 1970, one week earlier than expected". (37)

Three years later, in 1973, the character of the shore-sided part of the distillery was again changed when the vast industrial maltings were erected. Capable of producing 400 tonnes of malted barley each week, the maltings initially supplied only the three SMD distilleries Caol Ila, Lagavulin and Port Ellen, making their own floor maltings redundant. The replacement of the individual distillery maltings was necessary because the large scale malting plants produced with greater consistency and were also more economical. Apart from this, as distilleries were expanded during the 1960s and 70s, there was simply no way that the traditional floor maltings could keep up with the growing demand on malted barley. (38)
The Port Ellen floor maltings were closed in 1974 and became an engineering workshop and malt store. (39)
Water for mashing and distilling was still drawn from Leorin Lochs, where Diageo has water rights to this day (in fact, water from these lochs is exclusively used today by Port Ellen Maltings). The annual maximum production was 2,500,000 litres of alcohol. There were no silent seasons. Grant Carmichael thinks that Port Ellen produced around 1,700,000 litres of pure alcohol per year. (40)

Port Ellen malting floors

Destillation:
"There was nothing special about the cuts; thirty minutes of foreshots as far as I remember, and about four hours on spirit. We had no purifier; normal condensers. It was fine spirit – not as pungent as Laphroaig or Lagavulin."(41)
Maturation occurred on the premises in thirteen dunnage warehoues with a combined capacity of 10,000 casks. Because of the long closure of Port Ellen Distillery and the fact that no casks filled pre-1929 were left, many of the warehouses were used for maturing Malt Mill and Lagavulin casks.

Port Ellen
spirit safe

Port Ellen
stillhouse and spirit safe

The Port Ellen cask management was based on a twelve-year maturation period, using a mix of new and reused ex-bourbon casks and sherry butts. Grant Carmichael said: “We used more sherry butts than you get nowadays, up to 20 per cent I think, though the better butts always went to Lagavulin. And there was much less first-fill bourbon. There was even a shortage of casks back then, because overall production was so high; the filling strength went up to 68 or 69 per cent abv. for a few years.“ (42)

During the heydays, every cask was tapped on a rotating scheme by a workforce of three to trace spillage and leaks. It is said that it took two working days for these three men to check all the 10,000 casks.

Surviving Port Ellen casks are held at dunnage warehouses at the premises of the defunct Lochindaal Distillery, managed by Caol IIa. (43)

There are other rumours that the remaining Port Ellen casks were moved to Diageos central warehousing complexes on the mainland. Others say that the casks Diageo still owns are hidden in one of the Port Ellen warehouses.

Port Ellen loading of 1967 casks on lorry

FUJIFILM DOF

Port Ellen
stillhouse

FUJIFILM DOF

Port Ellen stills and condensers in 1969

Port Ellen and Brora

The old Clynelish Distillery was subsequently closed in May 1968, and the new distillery, now christened ‚Clynelish' so that it could benefit from the name's huge reputation, started producing one month later, in June 1968. Normally that could have been the end of the old Clynelish Distillery.

The summer of 1968 was very dry on Islay and Port Ellen ran out of water. As a result, it was feared that the ‚yield' of all DCL distilleries on Islay would fall short of the target by no less than 40,000 proof gallons. That would have been a big problem as Johnnie Walker's sales were growing fast at that time, and it had a lot of Islay malts in it's ‚recipes'. The DCL started to wonder whether it would be possible to produce heavily peated malt at other distilleries on the mainland, such as Clynelish. Some voices within the DCL suggested in October 1968 that the shortfall in the production could be reduced by installing new production facilities on Islay. Yet, it was decided that before considering any increase in facilities on the island, the possibility of producing an Islay type malt on the mainland, where the costs would be lower, should be examined.

From November 1968 on, DCL was discussing the peat level of the whisky, which was going to be produced and some trials were held at Port Dundas, while some were looking for an available distillery. Extended kilning finally produced a satisfactory result and the old Clynelish Distillery was chosen, with plans to start mashing in January 1969. Later on, DCL started to look for a new name and decided on ‚Brora' at a board meeting on December 2, 1969. From that moment on and up to 1973, Brora produced an extraordinary, heavily peated Islay-style malt. Yet, by July 1973, DCL had increased its production of Islay whiskies and there was no need to produce an Islay-type whisky at Brora Distillery anymore. (44)

The closure of Port Ellen Distillery Professor Ronnie Martin became managing director of Scottish Malt Distillers in 1979 and director of production of SMD's parent company, DCL. In 1982, the Scottish whisky industry was in great straits Overproduction and declining sales of blended whisky made it necessary to analyse the company's situation and to reduce production. When Professor Martin took over as director of production, the DCL had 45 malt distilleries of which 21 were subsequently closed. The Carsebridge Grain Distillery was closed as well as and many bonds vanished either.

Initially, the SMD officials looked at their portfolio and went to regroup it: A first group consisted of the modern distilleries or those that had recently undergone refurbishment. Here, measures to increase efficiency and cost-effectiveness were introduced. Another group comprised those distilleries that were desirable to be kept because of their quality and the strong demand for their products, e.g. whiskies for blenders throughout the industry, and bearing an importance to the companies' own blends. A third group consisted of the single malt whiskies with investment in the brands. (45)

What remained were the distilleries that SMD could do without - either a distillery that required a lot of capital spent on it, or one that no longer fitted the blender's requirements.

Caol Ila, Lagavulin and Port Ellen were all modern distilleries and did not require a lot of capital to be spent on them. Caol Ila was heavily rebuilt and modernized in 1972/73. It achieved the highest productivity and was extremely cost-efficient. Lagavulins stillhouse had been modernized in 1969. All four coal-fired stills – two of them from the former Malt Mill were taken out and replaced by four new steam-fired stills. (46) At this time its brand played an important role in the White Horse blend. Both malts were of some importance in promoting them as single malts.

Port Ellen was as modern as Lagavulin and the production capacity of both distilleries was nearly equal. Eventually, the blenders had the final say: Owing to its long closure period of forty years prior to 1967, the distillery had lost its importance for blenders, an importance it had enjoyed one hundred years before. Port Ellen whisky had been used in some famous blends, but in none as a defining ingredient.

An Old Guns blend was produced by Low Robertson & Co. Ltd., Leith, when they were licence holders of Port Ellen Distillery as part of Scottish Malt Distillers (SMD). It was a blended whisky sold mainly in Italy with Port Ellen was the prominent malt used. The brand was still around in the early „1980s“ but was discontinued following the creation of United Distillers Ltd. (47)

Low Robertson & Co. Ltd. and the SMD did not bottle Port Ellen as regular single malt. The decision to close Port Ellen Distillery was the result of this analysis. In March 1983, last fillings were done on site. For Lagavulin distillery it turned out to be a difficult time as well. Four jobs were lost out of a workforce of 20 and a four day week was in operation for some time. (48)

Between 1978 and 1983, Grant Carmichael was general manager of DCL/United Distillers three Islay Distilleries Caol Ila, Lagavulin and

Port Ellen, together with the new maltings at Port Ellen (that had been built in 1973/1974 at the same time the Caol Ila Distillery was rebuilt and enlarged).
Asked for the reason of the Port Ellen closure Carmichael remembered: "Twelve distilleries were closed on the mainland. So one had to go on Islay. It was a blender's decision really, and they closed Port Ellen rather than Caol Ila or Lagavulin. If Port Ellen had been on the go since 1967, remember the oldest whisky was only just approaching its sixteenth birthday. That made it something of an unproven quantity by comparison with the others" (49).
Carmichael confessed that it was the worst day in his life, when he had to tell the Port Ellen manager Angus MacTaggert and his staff in January 1983 that Port Ellen Distillery would cease to operate.
The message of the near closure of one of the Kildalton distilleries worried many people on Islay. In those days, DCL was well respected as an employer. The company had been renown for the good training and decent payment of its workforce, and such was the spirit that people would spend their entire working lives with DCL.

In a town with an unemployment rate of 20 per cent the local newspaper Illeach wrote: "There will be less draft so the farmers will suffer as will Willie Currie's haulage business. Mundell's transport will lose half a days work involved in taking malt from maltings to distillery, and two loads of whisky to the ferry per week. The loss of 20 distillery pay packets will be felt in the shops, pubs and service industries of Port Ellen." (50)

Luckily the analysis of the newspaper turned out to be partially wrong. Both DCL and Carmichael managed that no one would be laid off. Some of the Port Ellen staff members went for early retirement; the same arrangement applied for senior staff members at Caol Ila and Lagavulin. In the end everyone benefitted from a pension or another job. The well-known Lagavulin warehouse man Ian MacArthur was one of the Port Ellen workers, who found a new job at Lagavulin distillery.

Decline and Decay

After the closure in May 1983, Port Ellen Distillery was noted as mothballed. In fact, everything remained in place and fell into a state of disrepair. On a few occasions, the remains of the distillery were visited. The official guided tours were stopped in the late 1990s, when the corrosion had gone too far.

The East German Visit 1989

In late 1989, two East German whisky enthusiasts visited Port Ellen and managed to get inside the distillery; their impressions give an account of the state of the distillery six years after its closure.

In November 1989, immediately after the Berlin Wall had come down, the two friends from the Schwerin area, near the Baltic coast, used their newly gained freedom and went on a trip to Scotland by car. During their visit of the Isle of Islay, they also called at the Port Ellen Distillery which had then been shut down for half a decade.

They were shocked by the state of the distillery. The buildings were abandoned and some parts vandalized. It was clear to them that this distillery would never open again.

It appeared odd to them that everything in the distillery looked as if the work - just like in the fairy tale of Cinderella - had stopped the day before. Order books, purchase books, sales journal and tools were still lying around. They even stumbled across a full Port Ellen cask. Upon inspection of the cask's content, the two friends, to their dismay, discovered that it only contained foul-smelling water sadly. Because of their small-sized car they did not manage to take one of the four pot stills with them. Instead, they managed to get a SMD distillery stamp as a souvenir.

Port Ellen stillhouse and spirit safe in 1989

EB BDBG

In 1992, the license to distil whisky that was held by Low, Robertson & Co. was revoked.
The German whisky expert Walther Schobert visited the distillery in 1996. He seems to have been one of the last visitors having seen the four pot stills being in place.

Shortly after Schobert's visit, the stills had been removed.
In his newsletter Whisky Watch professor Schobert wrote that the stills had been brought to the famous still manufacturer Forsyth to be dismantled. Soon, other rumours about the stills having been sold and shipped to India occured.
Regarding the rumours about what had happened to the stills, Ingvar Ronde wrote in 2011: "The stills were shipped abroad early in the 1990s possibly destined for India..."(51)
No one officially will tell us the truth. Only Diageo could, but they have their special company secret.
It is true that an attempt to sell the stills to India failed in 1995. Members of the former Port Ellen workforce claim that the stills have been dismantled on site.

Visit in 1998

By the time another German Port Ellen enthusiast visited the distillery in 1998, the wash- and spirit-stills had all been removed. What he saw, were the black holes, where the stills had been admitted. He did not dare to venture inside the building, as he feared that the perforated plate covering of the roof could give way. 15 years had gone by since the closure of the distillery, and the signs of decay and corrosion were everywhere.

One of the eight washbacks had been removed from the tunroom and left to rot outside the distillery.

Turnbull Hutton, operations director of distillation and spirit supply of United Distillers & Vintners, the spirits section of Diageo's Guinness UDV, when asked in spring 2001 about the status of the Port Ellen Distillery: "The vandals have done a pretty good job and I would rather remove it but, we have a preservation order slapped on us "because it's got pagodas" - yes, corrugated-iron pagodas! It's a rundown eyesore of a place. As for selling it, we have a maltings sitting there, which is important to the island and having a distillery at the back owned by someone else doesn't make any sense. Lagavulin and Caol Ila are very important to us and I don't see any benefits for UDV in doing anything with Port Ellen other than tidying the site."
His wish for tidying most parts of the distillery site was fulfilled in March, April and May 2003.

Port Ellen washback, one missing in 1998

The End

On a beautiful sunny evening at the beginning of May 2003, three friends were taking the evening ferry from Kennacraig to Islay.

Upon their entering Port Ellen harbour, the distillery seemed unchanged. With the exception of the seaside Port-Ellen-lettering painted on the warehouses, everything appeared just the same as on their last visit back in 1996. However, everything had changed.

What they found at Port Ellen was a distillery in the process of being demolished. The heritage preservation that had been propagated over and over again obviously did not apply to the distillery proper, which had already been demolished completely. A wire fence sealed off the construction site. Two fence elements ,however, stood open for about one and a half metres. The friends asked one of the builders still on site, whether they would be allowed to look around and take some photos. The man nodded, but warned them to be particularly cautious because of hazardous debris. Then he finished his day's work and went away.

An excavator with 'Masterton' lettering, flooded with sunlight, contributed to an almost ghostly atmosphere.

The stillhouse was a place of total destruction. Only the four iron foundations for the stills remained intact. Everything else was dumped on a heap of debris a few metres further west.

The friends were taking a closer look at the other buildings that were still remaining. Through a window that was almost blind with dirt, they managed to photograph the Port Ellen malt mill, although only not entirely.

An open door enabled them to enter the demolished buildings. Via a flight of stairs they reached the mashtun that was still in place as well as its control equipment.

A yellow door led into the void. This was the spot, where the tunroom had once been, only identifiable by an inscription on a remaining wall.

Respectfully, and armed with two cameras, one of the friends ventured to climb to the next level via a flight of stairs, directly under an roof that was now gone. He was absolutely right to mistrust the stability of the steel steps that had been left to decay and corrode for twenty years, and that had furthermore been exposed to the vibrations of the demolition activities.

It was worth the risk, for he managed to take some shots through that were only possible to be taken at this stage of dismantling. Among these photos, there is one on which the twin pagodas can still be seen from inside the distillery. Only a few days later, the big red pagoda fell victim to the excavators.

Such, it was also possible to capture and preserve the image of both heritage-protected pagodas in a unique photograph.

Two days later the three friends returned for a last time.

By then, the demolition work had progressed even further, and as if the weather was reflecting this sad occasion, it was raining cats and dogs, amplifying the sentimental farewell atmosphere.

TUN ROOM

MASH TUN

WASH BACK

The Ileach wrote in Vol. 30 No.14 in 17 May 2003:

„As you will no doubt have noticed, the skyline around Port Ellen is currently changing as drinks company Diageo breathes new life into the old Port Ellen Distillery site.

Port Ellen Distillery ceased production in 1983 and the part of the distillery that was built in the 1960s had fallen into disrepair and was in a dangerous condition. Representatives from the drinks giant have spent considerable time in consultation with local groups, looking for the site and working towards a solution to benefit the whole community."

Group manager for Diageo´s Islay sites, Kay Fleming, said:"Rather than pour money away keeping the buildings wind and watertight, it was decided that the best solution for all concerned on Islay would be to demolish the unsafe part of the distillery and invest in the creation of starter-units, for development by local business and organisations. As well as the obvious economic benefit that this will bring, the amenity of the area will be greatly improved. The two older pagodas will be preserved and the red corrugated iron pagoda is no longer there, they have now become the more prominent feature. The derelict buildings have now been removed to reveal the original pagodas."(52)

The Remains:

The historically valuable and, hopefully, heritage-protected twin pagoda as well as the Port Ellen warehouses were preserved and remain next to the Port Ellen maltings that have been erected in 1973. It is particularly on the 'Open Day' during the Feis Ile that the Port Ellen Distillery is commemorated inside the maltings. Together with the Spirit Vat the last cask of Port Ellen filled in March 1983, has been preserved here. Right behind the cask, the iron letters from the Port Ellen Distillery have been fixed. The letter 'E', of 'Ellen', lost for many years, miraculously reappeared after the demolition.

According to official statements from Diageo, they wanted to offer local businesses and organisations a chance to settle on the old site. As a recent visit to the island in June 2014 has shown, a lot needs to be done. One of the protected pagodas desperately needs repairing, due to damage caused by the weather.

My wish is the establishment of a small museum inside the unused twin pagodas. During the „19th“ century the Port Ellen Distillery has, as already described, played an important role for the development of Scottish whisky production and its export, inter alia to the United States of America.

It seems, however, that even over 30 years after its shutdown, the time for a museum still does not appear to be ripe.

Port Ellen,
distillery and warehouse as seen from the shore in 2013

PORT ELLEN
DISTILLERY
LOW ROBERTSON & CO LTD

PORT ELLEN
ISLAY

PORT ELLEN

PORT ELLEN

WAREHOUSE 7

WAREHOUSE 3

When the Port Ellen Distillery was reactivated after nearly 40 years, there had naturally been no remaining casks from the time when operations were put to a halt. There is, however, one remarkable episode from the mid-"1980s". During the „1960s" and „1970s" DCL was using warehouses of the long-closed Hazelburn and Lochhead Distilleries in Campbeltown for storing Islay whisky, thereby yielding on a microclimate similar to that on Islay, while at the same time saving the cost for constructing new warehouses on the island.
Owing to the level of transport cost in the mid-1980ies, the warehouses were successively being emptied.
Grant Carmichael, who had been tasked to supervise vacating the warehouses, came across a quartercask of 1929 Port Ellen whisky in one of the Hazelburn stores. To his dismay, the cask contained only little whisky, which in addition had turned woody.

Owing to the shutdown period of its distillery from 1929 until 1966, the Port Ellen whisky brand did no longer enjoys the reputation it had 90 years ago. Due to the non-availability, other malts had substituted Port Ellen in the meantime.
The main reason for the re-equipment of the Port Ellen Distillery and its subsequent recommissioning by DCL was the company's demand for malt whisky from Islay for blending purposes during that period. During the operational years since 1967, Port Ellen malt has been mainly employed for blending (Blends:White Horse, J&B, Black&White).

During this short period, Port Ellen failed to reach the same importance as for instance Lagavulin malt in the White Horse blend or Ardbeg malt in the Ballentines blend. A small quantity of Port Ellen is said to have formed the basis malt in the Old Guns blend, which has mostly been sold in Italy.

It has been noted by Grant Carmichael, former general manager in charge of the DCL distilleries on Islay, that the oldest Port Ellen that has been produced was merely 16 years old. The distillery, newly opened in 1967, therefore had no chance to establish a status of its own before the beginning of the whisky crisis.

Whisky sales have been buoyant in the 1970s but began to stagnate. By 1980, industry stocks were equivalent to more than ten years' production. (53)
With the dwindling demand for whisky and the crisis looming on the horizon, the sales in blended whisky were, of course, stagnating as well. In those days, sales in malt whisky like today were only playing a very subordinate role in most companies

When the Port Ellen Distillery was shut down for good in 1983 in the course of measures to fight over production, its stores were well stocked, despite a considerably reduced output in 1982 and 1983. DCL, as the parent company, and its subsidiary SMD, responsible for the production, had closed down another ten distilleries apart from Port Ellen. The other remaining distilleries of the company were often producing at a considerably reduced rate.

When United Distillers took over DCL in 1987, the new proprietors not only took possession of the additional active and inactive DCL/SMD distilleries, but also their substantial warehouse stocks. After having analysed these stocks with regard to possible own needs, it can be assumed that their willingness to sell surplus casks to so-called third parties (brokers, independent bottlers) had increased.
It can therefore be taken for granted that next to selling to traditional customers from blending companies, larger quantities of Port Ellen casks have been sold to independent bottlers and brokers.
The situation at the time has been very well depicted in an interview with the founder and owner of James MacArthur Arthur Winning, by Brands & Cigar consultant Jens Tausch. Winning described the possibilities to acquire whisky casks in the „1980s" and „90s" as follows: "During that period, only very few independent bottlers existed, and it was no problem to acquire casks from distilleries like Ardbeg, Port Ellen or Caol Ila. There were few major players and it was much easier to deal with people than nowadays. Imagine, I just went into United Distillers in Edinburgh and was able to buy whatever I wanted. The motto was: 'You'll name it, we'll supply it.' As much Port Ellen and Caol Ila as I wanted."(54)

At a later stage, also new companies like Signatory vintage, founded in 1988, were profiting.
In 2002, Port Ellen expert Grant Carmichael commented on this issue: "Some of the independent bottlers are bottling the odd casks of Port Ellen from 1980 to 1982 and these must be a good buy at the moment."
In the beginning of 2002 Andrew Symington of Signatory Vintage succeeded in acquiring further 130 casks Port Ellen, mostly of 1978 and 1979 vintage from UDV/Diageo.
Since the beginning of the 1990ies, Port Ellen had already been available as single malt from specialised dealers in whiskies along with the bottlings from Gordon & MacPhail, Cadenhead and Signatory Vintage. Because of the excessive supply of casks, the Port Ellen brand was experiencing a revival as malt whisky among the so-called independents.

In 1998, brothers Fred and Stewart Laing began to offer own malts on the market next to their traditional blending business. Port Ellen had already been an important ingredient, when their father was running the business, for instance of the King of Sots blend. It was for this reason that they possessed substantial quantities in stock from this brand.
In the following five to seven years, the Laing brothers were flooding the malt whisky market, inter alia with numerous Ardbeg and even more diverse Port Ellen bottlings.

The analysis of casks by cask data

After more then thirty years of closure of the Port Ellen Distillery the stocks of Port Ellen are dwindling. It is nearly impossible to obtain some Port Ellen cask data because the leading companies which nowadays own the bulk of the remaining Port Ellen casks, Diageo and Douglas Laing, would never disclose their stock position.

Grant Carmichael has described the procedure at Port Ellen in 2002 in the following manner: „Each cask filled at the distillery at that time would have been stencilled with the year and a consecutive number starting with number 1 on 1st January. To my recollection the only private fillings at that time would have been for Gordon& Macphail." (54)

According to former Port Ellen staff, there have been no so-called 'silent seasons', i.e. operational breaks lasting several weeks on a regular basis

One such break that is known was a shortage of water during the summer of 1968. On 6 September 1968 the DCL production committee stated the following: "A serious water shortage on Islay had resulted in the closure of Port Ellen Distillery for two weeks and full production had only been resumed this week." (55)

Owing to the secrecy that many whisky companies kept and that will be explained at a later stage with regard to the Laing company, the only possibility is to analyse existing cask numbers as well as distilling and bottling dates. In this respect, the bottlings of Signatory Vintage, its secondary label Dun Eideann, G & M as well as of some independent bottlers, e.g. Old Bothwell, have shed some light on the darkness. This particularly applies to the ten initial production years of the Port Ellen Distillery; the cask numbers do rather resemble a jigsaw puzzle where most of the pieces have been lost forever. The same applies for the [exact] number of casks that were destined for blended whiskies. What has to be mentioned, is that the Port Ellen Distillery was filling the casks on site, which was a common practice at that time. In contrast to today's methods, the employment of bowsers transporting whisky in larger quantities to a larger filling facility was unheard of.

There is a complete lack of cask numbers from 1967 until 1973. The majority of the known

bottlings relates to the casks of 1969. The 1970 and 1971 vintages are again represented to a lesser degree. Until today, bottlings from 1972 and 1973 have not surfaced to this very day. A possible explanation for the lacking data for the last two vintages might be the fact that Caol Ila was undergoing a substantial reconstruction from April 1972 until January 1974 and could therefore not contribute any Islay malt for the whisky blends. Perhaps, Port Ellen casks from those vintages have substituted the Caol Ila malt in its blending role.

The first year that is somewhat telling with regard to casks that have been filled in the Port Ellen Distillery has been 1974. Such, a Port Ellen from the Signatory company, distilled on 30 November 1974, is carrying cask number 6756. It can therefore be assumed that the caskfillings had also been continuing in December of that year.

The year 1975 only offers an incomplete insight again. While on 14 January 1975 146 casks had already been filled, the data basis ends in April 1975 with a total of 1755 filled casks.

1976 is even less expressive. For that year, evidence is only retrievable for those casks that have been distilled in September by the Signatory, Dun Eideann and First Cask companies. The numbering of the casks starts at no. 4736 and ends with a cask strength filling from Signatory on 28 September 1976 at no. 4797. However, as in the previous year 1975 it also has to be assumed that production was running at full rate and therefore casks have also been filled until December.

For 1977, even less known cask numbers can be noted than in the year before. All casks that have been filled at Port Ellen can be traced for April, August and November.

While a cask strength filling by the Gordon & MacPhail company, marketed in August 1991, has the cask number 2017 (from 14 April 1977), there are two Port Ellen casks carrying cask numbers 3613 and 3615 for 19 August 1977. One cask, number 5569, filled on 11 November 1977 (by Dun Eideann) at least allows a comparison with the 1974 production. It can be assumed that the latter might have exceeded the 1977 production by some hundred casks.

For 1978, cask data from April, September and December are available. A high spirits filling from 1978 has cask number 6420.

The peak production year of the Port Ellen Distillery after its reopening in 1967 may have been 1979. For this year, cask numbers for the months of January, March, August, November and December can be traced. A Port Ellen with a distilling date of 11 December 1979, filled by G&M in the year 2000 (insert: photo label) consists of casks 7244 and 7247. A further cask, filled in December 1979 and bottled by John McDougall in his Golden Cask series, is even numbered 7983.

Unfortunately, it can by no means be concluded that the analysis of the „1980s“ cask production is any easier to accomplish. For the production year 1980, one cask number from March can be established, as well as others from August, one from September and furthermore a greater amount of numbers from November.

It appears that a production stop that lasted until August 1980 and that has been confirmed by former staff is the reason for this.

A cask that has been filled on 13 March 1980 carries number 1228. The next known numbered cask that can be traced has been filled in September 1980 and carries number 2562. It is known that distilling had recommenced as early as August 1980. But during this period cask identifications have been used that also Grant Carmichael was unable to explain.

Cask number 89/589/28 may serve as a reference example. This particular cask, filled on 6 August 1980, was bottled at the beginning of 1997 by The Ultimate. Further numbers with the identification 89/589/... have been notably bottled by the Signatory company and their sub label. Most likely, the counting runs from 89/589/1 to 89/589/48. The latter number is

the highest known cask number of a cask with this special counting that has been filled. The highest known "regular" number belongs to a 1997 bottling by G&M. The latter consisted of casks nos. 5101-5110 that have been distilled on 19 November 1980.

Thus the production, compared with the 1979 values, appeared to have dropped by approximately 2000 casks. This correlates with a statement given by Grant Carmichaels in 2002: "Production began to lessen from 1980 onwards culminating in closure of 11 DCL distilleries including of course Port Ellen in 1983." (56)

Facing overproduction and the crisis it entailed, the reduction of the Port Ellen production in the following years continued with an even more obvious trend. In this respect, particularly the 1981 vintage constitutes a challenge for the researcher. Isolated data exists for the months of April and Mai 1981. The two bottles, bottled by "The Bottlers" in 2000 relate to cask numbers 1549 and 1550 for the month of May.

At present, it remains widely unclear how many casks have eventually been filled in 1981 at Port Ellen because from May onwards no more fillings are known. It was only a Port Ellen cask from 1981 which has been photographed among a pile of empty casks of the Speyside Cooperage, that offered further hints. This cask had number 3345.

Three casks from Douglas Laing, bottled in 2000, give another indication. For reasons known, this company does not refer to cask numbers; the labels, however, refer to December 1981 as the date when the whisky was distilled.

Therefore, it can be taken as a fact that production had also continued during December 1981 and that the number of casks was in excess of cask no. 3345. At least former distillery staff has not confirmed that the 1981 production had decreased in comparison to the previous year.

The last two production years of the distillery are clearly indicating that production at Port Ellen had been considerably reduced. It can be assumed that in the year 1983 only some remaining casks were filled until the distillery was finally shut down. The fact that the available numbers carry more relevance with regard to their information is owing to the fact that those casks filled in 1982 and 1983 have been sold to independent customers and were therefore and still are bottled as single malt.

For 1982, data for Port Ellen casks from February, March, April, Mai, October, November and December is available.

It seems remarkable that the highest cask number was found on the inscription of a six pack of the "Provenance" series originating from Douglas Laing, consisting of a Port Ellen vintage distilled in December 1982. For this bottling cask numbers 3028, 3032 and 3034 were written on the packing tag. At least, the company secrecy of the Laings did no seem to be 100 per cent watertight in those days.

It occurs that the production of the Port Ellen Distillery was reduced considerably by 1982, a fact that is reflected in the number of casks that have been mentioned. It can be assumed that compared to 1980, they may have been halved.

Production in 1983 continued for only three months, before the distillery closed down for good. One of the last casks that has been filled may have been a sherry-butt, filled on 22 March 1983.
The last Port Ellen cask, filled in March 1983, numbered 839, nowadays remains at the Port Ellen Maltings and is on display next to the former spirit vat of the distillery.

The following conclusions can be drawn from this analysis of casks:
• The years 1974 and 1978/1979 have probably been the years of peak production at Port Ellen Distillery.
• Compared to the 1980 production figures, the annual production rate decreased by half until 1982.
• Obviously, so called 'series of casks' went on sale to independents, i.e. casks that were stored adjacent to each other in the warehouse were sold as a bundle. As an example, reference is made to the Signatory bottlings from 1979 casks numbered 5140, 5143 through 5148 and 5151 through 5154, or to the Ian Macleod company with the 1982 cask numbers 1512 through 1520.

What is still existing and what can still be expected?
For some years, market leader Diageo has realised that they can achieve a high publicity impact with their Annual and Special Releases, particularly from Port Ellen, Brora and Lagavulin. In spite of exorbitant price increases for the 12th ,13th and 14th Annual Release of a 32-, 34- and 35-year-old Port Ellen, financial aspects are not expected to play a role. That does not mean, however, that further price increases are going to follow suit.
The fact that the official Port Ellen bottlings always consist of a change of casks filled in 1979 and 1978 seems to indicate that United Distillers/Diageo still have stocks from those vintages. Both years have been strong to very strong production years of the distillery. Among them, 1979 had the highest known number of Port Ellen casks bottled.

At the end of 2009, Diageo had released a small hint with regard to still existing stocks for the first time.

Dr Morgan, Heritage Manager of Diageo, stated in an interview with Ingvar Ronde:
"I can confirm that we have limited supplies of Port Ellen, Brora and Rosebank in our inventory. Competition for these stocks between our blenders developing super premium products and the single malts team is very intense. But we will continue to bottle small quantities of Brora and Port Ellen as stocks allow ..." (57)
A lot of leeway for speculation remains regarding what 'limited supplies' means from the mouth of an executive of industry leader Diageo. It is a fact that Diageo issued their 10th, 11th and 12th Annual Release with a total number of 15 000 bottles.
On the occasion of the 12th Annual Release of a 32 year old Port Ellen in summer 2012, the same Nick Morgan, meanwhile Diageo's head of whisky outreach, stated:
"And our ever-diminishing stocks of Brora and Port Ellen have once again been successfully explored for hidden treasures, which will no doubt further increase the huge over-demand for these rare products. It is amazing to think that those distilleries closed nearly 30 years ago."
Despite the 'limited supply', Diageo appears to still be in the possession of Port Ellen stock. The 14th Annual Release for 2014 was delivered in October 2014.
The competition with the blenders seems to have been decided in favour of the single malt bottlings, as long as the 35- to 36-year-old casks are of an appropriate quality. There are rumours that Diageo wants to set some stocks aside for a 40-year-old Port Ellen.
In October 2013 Dr. Morgan was asked the typical question in an American whiskycast: "How much more (Port Ellen) you have left in the warehouses?"
Morgan answered in his usual fashion: "We never discuss our inventory position. It is quite clear we do not have a lot left. We reduced the (.....) bottling by half. We did (...) a couple of years ago just to make sure we got a little bit longer with it. We are very lucky at the moment that the quality is being maintained and that is the really important thing and not how old the stuff is."
"It is whether it is still good enough to put it in the bottle. And at the moment we have our fingers crossed to make sure we are still in that position."
"If we are, than we got a few years to go, but it is like everything else like you and me Mark, one day we're no longer be here." (58)
"All we got is the point when the quality is not good enough for a single malt bottling."
"Whiskies that are not necessarily 100% for Single Malt bottling, can be 100% for the blends."
At about the same time, Dr Morgan uttered in The Guardian: "We are down to our last few casks. In a decade or so, it might all be gone". (59)
It seems to me, as if quality and quantity of the remaining Port Ellen casks is still sufficient. And this could continue for the years to come.
It is remarkable that Diageo, on the occasion of the Islay Festival in 2008 has bottled cask number 1301 that had been filled in 1981. Should there be a greater quantity of secretly hidden stock of 1981 vintage? There are many indications that this is the case.

Fred Laing, for instance, remarked in December 2012:
"No, strangely enough we do not have any 1981 PE." This means that presently the Laing company no longer has any 1981 casks.
(60)
Deducting from the Festival bottling of a Port Ellen cask distilled in 1981, it seems to be more than probable that Diageo possibly still hoards considerable numbers of casks from that year. A hidden reserve, if the stocks of 1978 and 1979 distilled Port Ellen whisky should finish or their quality diminish.

Also, no argument can be found against the assumption that in this event Diageo could repurchase or acquire by exchange. It has been particularly this scheme that independent bottling sources have referred to. In 2012, Diageo was said to have massively rebought casks from Port Ellen, but also from Caol Ila. This is obviously also a matter of prestige. It is nearly impossible for independent bottlers to acquire a Port Ellen cask at all. Apart from the massively increased cask prices there is an ever-growing financially potent competition from Asia.
The primary addressee for a repurchase could have been the Laing brother's company who, next to Diageo, should have had the largest stock. A further target could have been the Old Bothwell company that after 25 bottlings had allegedly used up their Port Ellen casks. At least older vintages which – next to the known casks, filled in 1982 and 1983- were still in Old Bothwell's possession in February 2011, might have found their way to Diageo.

Meanwhile, in August 2015, Diageo announced the 15th Annual release of a Port Ellen. Surprisingly, this bottling is a vatting of casks that were distilled in 1983. It is "only" 32 years old and has a strength of 53,9%. The number of bottles is 2964.
This could mean that the stocks of 1978 and 1979 distilled Port Ellen have no longer the needed quality or that there are insuffiicent good quality casks from those years and/or those remaining casks are reserved for a 40-year-old original bottling in 2018 or 2019.
Competitors of Douglas Laing's commented upon Diageo's stocks and sale policies as follows:
"We cannot believe that Diageo sold nearly all 1982/83 Port Ellen distillation to independent bottlers. My understanding is that their ability to release new additions means they held a lot of stock. It is a little surprising, however, that our own oldest Port Ellen stock (1977) is 35 years – somewhat older than Diageo seem able to release."(61)

For the reasons given in that statement, the author cannot endorse the cask analysis of a Canadian Port Ellen enthusiast on the probable Diageo stocks dating from May 2011. Regarding the number of bottlings that actually have been produced at Diageo's until the end of 2013, the estimated figure of 40 casks, predominantly from 1978 and 1979, has definitely proven to be too low.
My own hypothesis is that Diageo still has a stock in excess of 300 casks. These are supposedly composed of 1978, 1979, 1980, 1981, 1982 and 1983 vintage.

A single still topped up Port Ellen cask from 1980 rests in the so-called Ultima Warehouse at the Diageo Distillery Knockando.

Professor Walther Schobert, a renown German Port Ellen expert, stated in his latest work: "In the meantime, one or the other independent [bottler] might regret how lavishly they have drawn on their stocks, although there are enough remaining casks and therefore, the hype is ultimately not justified!"(62)

Apart from Douglas Laing and Hunter Laing some Port Ellen casks remain in storage with other independent companies, e.g. Malts of Scotland in Germany, Duncan Taylor (mainly casks from 1983) and Macillops. One should not forget Gordon MacPhail, who still own casks of many lost distilleries and are renown for the age and the quality of their cask stocks. Especially this company had started to ration their Port Ellen bottlings years ago.
Furthermore, I presume that Sukhinder Singh and his company are also in possession of some Port Ellen casks.
Three years ago, Signatory vintage declared to visitors of the Edradour Distillery, that only two Port Ellen casks were left. This however is a statement that I would not subscribe to.
In my opinion some companies will surprise us with a 40-year-old Port Ellen in the next five years.

Port Ellen bottlings

As Sukhinder Singh wrote in 2007: "Port Ellen is a versatile malt, with considerable differences of style evident between different bottlings. Some sherry-casked Port Ellen can be beautifully rich, spicy, sweet and leathery; bourbon and refill casks often show a more austere, peppery medium-weighted style. Common characteristics, though, are a high level of peatiness and, in the best examples, a phenomenal complexity which Islay fans adore."
Port Ellen was closed in the slump of 1983, but the whisky made in the 16 years between its re-opening and the final closure has gained a reputation as being some of the finest that has been made on Islay in that time. Originally designed for blending, it was not very complicated, when it was young and filled into Bourbon casks. In many ten-year-old bottlings one will find a good sweetness and peatiness, a lot of pepper as well as some parsley and spice. All in all it is clean, uncomplicated and very drinkable.

As Grand Carmichael noted, after about 18 years Port Ellen Malt takes on a soft, chocolaty flavour. One of the early Douglas Laing Provenance bottlings with 18 years is a good example for this.
It is proven that Port Ellen filled in casks with good quality can be stored for more than 30 years. Then, as Sukhinder Singh describes, the malt develops a phenomenal complexity. All of the annual releases, which I could afford to taste (No. 1-12) had kept its quality.

Price changes

Bottler	Name	Age	Description	Strength	Size	Price £
	PORT ELLEN		(ISLAY / DEMOLISHED)			
RM	Port Ellen 1978	22		60.5%	70cl	69.00
RM	Port Ellen 1978 #	20		60.9%	70cl	89.00
ARN	Port Ellen 1982	17	ARN - Acorn (Japan)	62.6%	70cl	100.00
CC	Port Ellen 1981-2000	19		40%	70cl	50.00
CC	Port Ellen 1981-1999	18		40%	70cl	55.00
CC	Port Ellen 1980-1997	17		40%	70cl	65.00
COP	Port Ellen 1981	18		43%	70cl	85.00
CRT	Port Ellen 1969	24	Sherrywood	40%	70cl	175.00
CSK	Port Ellen 1979	20		60.7%	70cl	92.50
CSK	Port Ellen 1979	19		61.1%	70cl	99.00
DL	Port Ellen 1982	18	Sherrywood / Jan 2001	50%	70cl	55.00
DL	Port Ellen 1981	19	Sherrywood / Dec 2000	50%	70cl	59.00
DL	Port Ellen 1979	21	Bottled Dec 2000	50%	70cl	63.00
DL	Port Ellen 1979	21	Bottled July 2000	50%	70cl	75.00
DL	Port Ellen 1979	21	Bottled Feb 2001	50%	70cl	65.00
DL	Port Ellen 1979	21	Sherrywood / Feb' 2001	50%	70cl	68.00
DL	Port Ellen 1978	22	Bottled Feb 2001	50%	70cl	68.00
DL	Port Ellen 1976	24	Bottled Dec 2000	50%	70cl	69.75
LBD	Port Ellen 1982	18	Jewels of Islay	50%	70cl	75.00
MG	Port Ellen 1982	18	Bottled Spring 2001	43%	70cl	47.00
MM	Port Ellen 1982	17		46%	70cl	80.00
SIG	Port Ellen 1975 "2000"	24	Cask No.1769	43%	70cl	65.00
SIG	Port Ellen 1976	22	Cask No.4755	55.4%	70cl	80.00
SIG	Port Ellen 1976	22	Cask No.4756	55.9%	70cl	80.00
SIG	Port Ellen 1976	22	Cask No.4760	58.8%	70cl	80.00
SIG	Port Ellen 1976	23	Cask No.4762	58%	70cl	69.00
SIG	Port Ellen 1976	22	Cask No.4749	56.2%	70cl	80.00
SIG	Port Ellen 1980	17	Cask No.89 / 589 / 38	59.5%	70cl	85.00
SAM	Port Ellen 1975	23		45%	70cl	120.00
STE	Port Ellen 1974	15	Black Glass	40%	75cl	175,00
STE	Port Ellen 1979	16	Shield Shape Label	40%	70cl	130.00
ULT	Port Ellen 1977	16	Cask No.5559	43%	70cl	POA

Revised price list, TheWhiskyExchange, 2001

As per 2015, the market for Port Ellen is somewhat swept. Only few merchants, like Sukhinder Singh of TheWhiskyExchange and purveyors in rarities, continue to have more comprehensive supplies. They are asking quite ambitious prices for thes, of course.

For a couple of years, the annual releases have been dominating sales platforms like eBay. With the exception of the first release that is rarely ever sold by auction, all releases up to the 14th are being hawked.

The price for the formerly quite reasonably priced 2nd to 8th release has in the meantime levelled off at £ 650. New independent fillings, as for instance Duncan Taylor, Douglas Laing, or Gordon & MacPhail remain on the market as well because they already entered it at prices ranging from £500 to £1,000.

This development may have been instigated by the massive price increases that DIAEGO had announced for their 12th and 13th, but particularly the 14th release. Needless to say that it had not gone unnoticed to the proprietor of the Port Ellen rights, how the struggle for allotments and price rigging around the 11th release, comprising 3 000 bottles, had evolved. The attempt to regulate the market by nearly doubling the price for the 12th release failed, although in quantity it only fell a few bottles short of its predecessor. Subsequently, the prices for the 13th and 14th release were increased even more substantially, also on grounds of rarity. While in the beginning £1,600 were asked for a 13th release bottle, the price for the 35 year old 14th release has been increased to a hefty £2,200 during the last quarter of 2014.
In contrast, the development regarding the older bottlings surprises. Having been disregarded for many years – a Signatory-Millenium bottling from 1975 could until recently be acquired for much less than £ 200 – a constant increase in prices has now begun. Owing to the exorbitant price increases of the most recent bottlings, parts of the market are heading for the inexpensive ones that have entered the market years ago. Nevertheless, some Port Ellen bottlings still remain being underrated.
A further booster for the Port Ellen bottlings from the last decade are the high ratings by whisky connoisseurs as for instance the Malt-Maniacs. Such, a rating of 95 out of 100 possible points, for instance, will guarantee a swift sale of the bottles and a considerably higher margin of profit. This also applies to the Port Ellen Rare Malts after they have been easily available for nearly a decade. The 22-year-old Rare Malt, rated at 93 points, presently sells at around £750.
On his homepage British Port Ellen expert and renown whisky merchant Sukhinder Singh commented the development of prices in November 2011 as follows:
"Two things are certain: The market price of previous years' official releases is almost certain never to go down, while prices of future distillery bottlings will increase further. The 1st release from 2001 started life at £110; today the retail price would be around £1,000.
There are also some casks of Port Ellen still with independent bottlers, but with the speed of sales I cannot see these lasting too many more years. Also, with every new release we see an increase in price: the average price of a cask strength Port Ellen was about £50 in 2002; as we reach the end of 2011, it is around £180-200."
Because of the recent price explosions this estimate is now outdated. The Port Ellen 1st release meanwhile costs more than £2,000. There are no more cask strength Port Ellen bottlings on sale for a price below £300.
Sukhinder Singh's maxim, that official bottlings never go down in price, will always remain valid.
It can be concluded, however, that since the massive price increase for the 13th, 14th and 15th release has occurred, those bottlings will remain longer on the merchants' shelves than the preceding releases. Many Port Ellen collectors have withdrawn from this segment, and therefore, due to the reduced number of customers, the situation for venturers will clearly become more difficult.

Port Ellen,
12-year-old whisky bottled for Queen Elizabeth II

RARE MALTS
SELECTION
NATURAL
CASK STRENGTH
SINGLE MALT
SCOTCH WHISKY
AGED 20 YEARS
DISTILLED 1978
PORT ELLEN
DISTILLERY
ESTABLISHED 1825
ISLE OF ISLAY
60.90%vol 70cle
PRODUCED AND BOTTLED
IN SCOTLAND
LIMITED EDITION
BOTTLE № 7492
OCTOBER 1998
RARE MALTS
SELECTION
NATURAL
CASK STRENGTH
SINGLE MALT
SCOTCH WHISKY
AGED 22 YEARS
DISTILLED 1978
PORT ELLEN
DISTILLERY
ESTABLISHED 1825
ISLE OF ISLAY
60.50%vol 70cle
PRODUCED AND BOTTLED
IN SCOTLAND
LIMITED EDITION
BOTTLE № 2717
OCTOBER 2000

RARE MALTS
SELECTION
NATURAL
CASK STRENGTH
SINGLE MALT
SCOTCH WHISKY
AGED 20 YEARS
DISTILLED 1978
PORT ELLEN
DISTILLERY
ESTABLISHED 1825
ISLE OF ISLAY
60.90%vol 70cle
PRODUCED AND BOTTLED
IN SCOTLAND
LIMITED EDITION
BOTTLE No 7492
OCTOBER 1998
Port Ellen Maltings
1973
1998
For twenty five years Port Ellen Maltings has supplied the finest malt to the Islay & Jura Distilleries. This anniversary bottling made with heavily peated malt is an excellent example and fitting tribute to the skill of the people who worked there over the years.
PORT ELLEN
58.4%vol Aged 21 Years 70cle
RARE MALTS
SELECTION
NATURAL
CASK STRENGTH
SINGLE MALT
SCOTCH WHISKY
AGED 22 YEARS
DISTILLED 1978
PORT ELLEN
DISTILLERY
ESTABLISHED 1825
ISLE OF ISLAY
60.50%vol 70cle
PRODUCED AND BOTTLED
IN SCOTLAND
LIMITED EDITION
BOTTLE No 2717
OCTOBER 2000

RELEASE
NATURAL CASK STRENGTH SINGLE MALT WHISKY
ESTABLISHED. 1825
PORT ELLEN
PORT ELLEN DISTILLERY
PORT ELLEN, ISLE OF ISLAY PA12 7AJ
Limited Edition Numbered Bottle No. 4010
One of only 9000 bottled in 2003
Distilled in 1979. Aged 24 Years
57.3% vol 70cl e
2nd RELEASE
NATURAL CASK STRENGTH SINGLE MALT WHISKY
ESTABLISHED. 1825
PORT ELLEN
PORT ELLEN DISTILLERY
PORT ELLEN, ISLE OF ISLAY PA12 7AJ
Limited Edition Numbered Bottle No. 7091
One of only 12000 bottled in 2002
Distilled in 1978. Aged 24 Years
Matured and Bottled by the Distillers
59.35% vol 70cl e
NATURAL CASK STRENGTH SINGLE MALT WHISKY
ESTABLISHED. 1825
PORT ELLEN
PORT ELLEN DISTILLERY
PORT ELLEN, ISLE OF ISLAY PA12 7AJ
Limited Edition Numbered Bottle No. 1646
One of only 6000 bottled in 2001
Distilled in 1979. Aged 22 Years
56.2% vol 70cl e

4TH RELEASE
NATURAL CASK STRENGTH SINGLE MALT WHISKY
ESTABLISHED. 1825
PORT ELLEN
PORT ELLEN DISTILLERY
PORT ELLEN, ISLE OF ISLAY PA12 7AJ
Limited Edition Numbered Bottle No. 4762
Distilled in 1978. Aged 25 Years
56.2% vol 70cle
5TH RELEASE
NATURAL CASK STRENGTH SINGLE MALT WHISKY
ESTABLISHED. 1825
PORT ELLEN
ISLAY SINGLE MALT SCOTCH WHISKY
PORT ELLEN DISTILLERY
PORT ELLEN, ISLE OF ISLAY PA12 7AJ
Limited Edition Numbered Bottle No. 4581
Distilled in 1979. Aged 25 Years
57.4% vol 70cle
6TH RELEASE
NATURAL CASK STRENGTH SINGLE MALT WHISKY
ESTABLISHED. 1825
PORT ELLEN
ISLAY SINGLE MALT SCOTCH WHISKY
PORT ELLEN DISTILLERY
PORT ELLEN, ISLE OF ISLAY PA12 7AJ
Limited Edition Numbered Bottle No. 1437
Distilled in 1978. Aged 27 Years
54.2% vol 70cle

SEVENTH 7 RELEASE
NATURAL CASK STRENGTH SINGLE MALT WHISKY
ESTABLISHED. 1825
PORT ELLEN
ISLAY SINGLE MALT SCOTCH WHISKY
PORT ELLEN DISTILLERY
PORT ELLEN, ISLE OF ISLAY PA12 7AJ
Limited Edition Numbered Bottle No. 2055
Distilled in 1979. Aged 28 Years
53.8% vol 70cl e
EIGHTH 8 RELEASE
NATURAL CASK STRENGTH SINGLE MALT WHISKY
ESTABLISHED. 1825
PORT ELLEN
ISLAY SINGLE MALT SCOTCH WHISKY
PORT ELLEN DISTILLERY
PORT ELLEN, ISLE OF ISLAY PA12 7AJ
ANNUAL RELEASE
Limited Edition Bottle No. 0305
One of only 6618 bottled in 2008
Distilled in 1978. Aged 29 years
Matured and Bottled by the Distillers
55.3% vol 70cl e
NINTH 9TH RELEASE
NATURAL CASK STRENGTH SINGLE MALT WHISKY
ESTABLISHED. 1825
PORT ELLEN
ISLAY SINGLE MALT SCOTCH WHISKY
PORT ELLEN DISTILLERY
PORT ELLEN, ISLE OF ISLAY PA12 7AJ
ANNUAL RELEASE
Limited Edition Bottle No. 2492
One of only 5916 bottled in 2009
Distilled in 1979. Aged 30 years
Matured and Bottled by the Distillers
57.7% vol 70cl e
30 YEARS OLD

TENTH 10th RELEASE
NATURAL CASK STRENGTH SINGLE MALT WHISKY
ESTABLISHED. 1825
PORT ELLEN
ISLAY SINGLE MALT SCOTCH WHISKY
PORT ELLEN DISTILLERY
PORT ELLEN, ISLE OF ISLAY PA12 7AJ
ANNUAL RELEASE
Limited Edition Bottle No. 2211
One of only 3000 bottled in 2010
Distilled in 1978. Aged 31 years
Matured and Bottled by the Distillers
54.6% vol 70cl
31 YEARS OLD
ELEVENTH 11th RELEASE
NATURAL CASK STRENGTH SINGLE MALT WHISKY
ESTABLISHED. 1825
PORT ELLEN
ISLAY SINGLE MALT SCOTCH WHISKY
PORT ELLEN DISTILLERY
PORT ELLEN, ISLE OF ISLAY PA12 7AJ
ANNUAL RELEASE
Limited Edition Bottle No. 0908
One of only 2988 bottled in 2011
Distilled in 1979. Aged 32 years
Matured and Bottled by the Distillers
53.9% vol 70cl
32 YEARS OLD
TWELFTH 12th RELEASE
NATURAL CASK STRENGTH SINGLE MALT WHISKY
ESTABLISHED. 1825
PORT ELLEN
ISLAY SINGLE MALT SCOTCH WHISKY
PORT ELLEN DISTILLERY
PORT ELLEN, ISLE OF ISLAY PA12 7AJ
ANNUAL RELEASE
Limited Edition Bottle No. 2123
One of only 2964 bottled in 2012
Distilled in 1979. Aged 32 years
Matured and Bottled by the Distillers
52.5% vol 70cl
32 YEARS OLD

THIRTEENTH 13th RELEASE
NATURAL CASK STRENGTH SINGLE MALT WHISKY
ESTABLISHED. 1825
PORT ELLEN
ISLAY SINGLE MALT SCOTCH WHISKY
PORT ELLEN DISTILLERY
PORT ELLEN, ISLE OF ISLAY PA12 7AJ
ANNUAL RELEASE
Limited Edition Bottle No. 1917
One of only 2958 bottled in 2013
Distilled in 1978. Aged 34 years
Matured and Bottled by the Distillers
55% vol 70cl e
34 YEARS OLD

FOURTEENTH 14th RELEASE
NATURAL CASK STRENGTH SINGLE MALT WHISKY
ESTABLISHED. 1825
PORT ELLEN
ISLAY SINGLE MALT SCOTCH WHISKY
PORT ELLEN DISTILLERY
PORT ELLEN, ISLE OF ISLAY PA12 7AJ
ANNUAL RELEASE
Limited Edition Bottle No.
One of only 2964 bottled in 2011
Distilled in 1978 Aged 35 years
Matured and Bottled by the Distillers
56.5% vol 70cl e
35 YEARS OLD

Bottle No. 0026
NATURAL CASK STRENGTH SINGLE MALT WHISKY
ESTABLISHED. 1825
PORT ELLEN
ISLAY SINGLE MALT SCOTCH WHISKY
PORT ELLEN DISTILLERY
PORT ELLEN, ISLE OF ISLAY PA12 7AJ
BOTTLED ESPECIALLY FOR FEIS ILE 2008
DATE FILLED 15/04/1981
Distilled in April 1981. Bottled in 2008
EX REFILL AMERICAN OAK
Cask No. 1301
54.7% vol 70cl e
BOTTLED ESPECIALLY FOR FEIS ILE 2008
BOTTLED ESPECIALLY FOR FEIS ILE 2008

NATURAL CASK STRENGTH
Islay single malt
SCOTCH WHISKY
PORT ELLEN
aged 15 years
DISTILLED IN 1969
MATURED AND BOTTLED IN 1985 BY
GORDON & MACPHAIL
ELGIN SCOTLAND
75 cl
64.7% vol
PORT ELLEN
Islay single malt
SCOTCH WHISKY
Acquavite di Cereali
DISTILLED 1969 DISTILLED
BOTTLED 1985
Imbottigliato Da
MATURED AND BOTTLED BY
GORDON & MACPHAIL
ELGIN · SCOTLAND
Importato da Meregalli Monza
Licenza U.T.I.F. 49 Milano
40%vol
75cl
PRODUCT OF SCOTLAND
PRODUCT OF SCOTLAND
Connoisseurs Choice
15 YEARS OLD
Scotch
Pure Malt Whisky
FROM THE
Port Ellen
Distillery, Islay
Proprietors: Low Robertson & Co. Ltd.
Distilled 1969
75 cl
40% vol
BOTTLED IN SCOTLAND BY
GORDON & MACPHAIL · ELGIN · SCOTLAND

AGED 18 YEARS
CONNOISSEURS CHOICE
SINGLE ISLAY MALT SCOTCH WHISKY
DISTILLED AT
PORT ELLEN
DISTILLERY
DISTILLED 1970 DISTILLED
GORDON & MACPHAIL
PRODUCT OF SCOTLAND
Distilled 1970
Bottled 1989
40° vol
PORT ELLEN
years 19 old
Islay Malt
Scotch Whisky
75 cl
Product of Scotland from Port Ellen Distillery - Islay
PORT ELLEN
Islay Single Malt
SCOTCH WHISKY
DISTILLED 1971 DISTILLED
BOTTLED 1990
Matured & Bottled By
Gordon & MacPhail
Elgin, Scotland
40%vol
75cl
PRODUCT OF SCOTLAND

PRODUCT OF SCOTLAND
Distilled 1974
Bottled 1988
43° vol
PORT ELLEN
years 14 old
Islay Malt
Scotch Whisky
75 cl
Product of Scotland from Port Ellen Distillery - Islay
PRODUCT OF SCOTLAND
Distilled 1974
Bottled 1988
65,5° vol
PORT ELLEN
years 14
Islay Malt
Scotch Whisky
75 cl
Product of Scotland from Port Ellen Distillery

The "Van Gogh" Collection
The
Port Ellen
Single Islay Malt Scotch Whisky
guaranteed 24 years old
Product of Scotland from Port Ellen Distillery
Matured in Sherry Wood
Selected and bottled in exclusivity for
70 cl
CARATO
40%
The "Van Gogh" Collection
The
Port Ellen
Single Islay Malt Scotch Whisky
guaranteed 16 years old
Product of Scotland from Port Ellen Distillery
Matured in Sherry Wood
Selected and bottled in exclusivity for
70 cl
CARATO
40%

Vintage 1974
Single Malt Scotch Whisky
SIGNATORY VINTAGE SCOTCH WHISKY CO. LTD.
Matured in oak casks for 17 years
Distilled at the Port Ellen Distillery
70cl
43%vol
Signatory Vintage Scotch Whisky
Vintage 1974
Single Islay Malt Scotch Whisky
Matured in oak casks for 17 years
Distilled at the Port Ellen Distillery
70cl
43%vol
Vintage 1974
Single Islay Malt Scotch Whisky
Matured in oak casks for 18 years
Distilled at the Port Ellen Distillery
70cl
ISLAY SINGLE MALT SCOTCH WHISKY
1974
PORT ELLEN
BOTTLED BY HAND
70cl
46%vol

SIGNATORY
VINTAGE
CASK STRENGTH COLLECTION
ISLAY SINGLE MALT SCOTCH WHISKY
PORT ELLEN
1974
AGED 30 YEARS
Distilled on: 30/11/1974
Bottled on: 31/08/2005
Matured in a Hogshead
Cask No: 6756
Bottle No: 67 of 266
NATURAL COLOUR
70cl 58.5%vol
Casks individually selected and bottled by Signatory Vintage Scotch Whisky Co. Ltd Edinburgh EH6 5PY
PRODUCT OF SCOTLAND
SIGNATORY
VINTAGE
ISLAY SINGLE MALT SCOTCH WHISKY
1974
PORT ELLEN
BOTTLED BY HAND
Aged: 30 years
Matured in: Hogshead
Distilled on: 30/11/1974
Cask No: 6757
Bottled on: 5/10/2005
Bottle: 49 of 235
70cl 46%vol
Selected and Bottled by
Signatory Vintage Scotch Whisky Co.Ltd. Edinburgh EH6 5PY Scotland

Silent Stills
Single Islay Malt Scotch Whisky
22 YEARS OLD
Distilled at
PORT ELLEN DISTILLERY
Distilled 30.11.74 Bottled 15.5.97
Cask No 6754 Bottle No 195 of 260
70cl 59.2%vol
Bottled in Scotland by
Signatory Vintage Scotch Whisky Co. Ltd. Edinburgh EH6 5PY
Silent Stills
Single Islay Malt Scotch Whisky
23 YEARS OLD
Distilled at
PORT ELLEN DISTILLERY
Distilled 14.1.75 Bottled 5.6.98
Cask No 160 Bottle No 98 of 285
70cl 56.1%vol
Bottled in Scotland by
Signatory Vintage Scotch Whisky Co. Ltd. Edinburgh EH6 5PY
Silent Stills
Single Islay Malt Scotch Whisky
18 YEARS OLD
Distilled at
PORT ELLEN DISTILLERY
Distilled 16.1.79 Bottled 29.10.97
Cask No. 274 Bottle No. 70 of 190
70cl 56.3%vol
Bottled in Scotland by
Signatory Vintage Scotch Whisky Co. Ltd. Edinburgh EH6 5PY

Scotch Single Malt
Port Ellen
Specially selected for
Scotch Single Malt Circle
Date destilled: 07.11.74
Date bottled: Mrz. '93
Proof stregth: 98.8° 56.4%
Volume: 70 cl
Distilled, matured and bottled in Scotland
Cask No. 6206
Scotch Single Malt
Port Ellen
Specially Selected for
Scotch Single Malt Circle
Date distilled: 04. 10. '82
Date bottled: February '95
Proof strength: 64.1% vol
Volume: 70cl
Distilled, matured and bottled in Scotland
Cask No 2376
Scotch Single Malt
Port Ellen
distilled at Port Ellen Distillery
Specially selected for
Scotch Single Malt Circle
Date distilled: Nov. 1982
Date bottled: März 2003
Proof strength: 61,2 %
Volume: 0,7 cl
Distilled, matured and bottled in Scotland
distilled at Port Ellen Distillery
Single Malt Scotch Whisky
Specially selected by
distilled, matured & bottled in Scotland
Date distilled: January 1983
Date bottled: March 2008
Strength: 58,4 % vol.
Volume: 70 cl
Cask-No.: 2542 refill Sherry
Bottle No. 25 of 247
Product of Scotland
www.scotchsingle.de

WILSON & MORGAN BARREL SELECTION
12
YEARS OLD
SINGLE MALT SCOTCH WHISKY FROM
PORT ELLEN
DISTILLERY
70 cl e
WILSON & MORGAN BARREL SELECTION
15
YEARS OLD
SINGLE MALT SCOTCH WHISKY FROM
PORT ELLEN
DISTILLERY
DISTILLED 1980
BOTTLED 1996
BOTTLED BY WILSON & MORGAN EDINBURGH SCOTLAND
70 cl. e
WILSON & MORGAN BARREL SELECTION
18
YEARS OLD
SINGLE MALT SCOTCH WHISKY FROM
PORT ELLEN
DISTILLERY
DISTILLED 1976
BOTTLED BY WILSON & MORGAN EDINBURGH SCOTLAND
70 cl. e

WILSON & MORGAN BARREL SELECTION
23
YEARS OLD
SINGLE MALT SCOTCH WHISKY
FROM
PORT ELLEN
DISTILLERY
DISTILLED 1975
BOTTLED FOR
WILSON & MORGAN
EDINBURGH SCOTLAND
CASK STRENGTH
vol. 59.1%
70 cl. e
WILSON & MORGAN BARREL SELECTION
16
YEARS OLD
SINGLE MALT SCOTCH WHISKY
FROM
PORT ELLEN
DISTILLERY
DISTILLED 1977
BOTTLED BY
WILSON & MORGAN
EDINBURGH SCOTLAND
CASK STRENGTH
vol. 56.6%
70 cl. e
WILSON & MORGAN BARREL SELECTION
TwentyThree
YEARS OLD
DISTILLED 1979
BOTTLED 2002
Port Ellen
DISTILLERY
BOTTLED FOR
WILSON&MORGAN EDINBURGH
SCOTLAND
BUTT N.5538
70cl. e 46% vol.

DISTILLED MAY 1981
19
Years Old
JULY 2000
BOTTLED AT CASK STRENGTH
THE BOTTLERS
FINE SINGLE ISLAY
SCOTCH MALT WHISKY
from Port Ellen Distillery
Cask No
1549
Cask Type - Refill Sherry Butt
Distilled and Bottled in Scotland
70cl
DISTILLED MAY 1981
19
Years Old
JULY 2000
BOTTLED AT CASK STRENGTH
THE BOTTLERS
FINE SINGLE ISLAY
SCOTCH MALT WHISKY
from Port Ellen Distillery
Cask No
1550
Cask Type - Refill Sherry Butt
Distilled and Bottled in Scotland
70cl
DISTILLED MAR 1979
22
Years Old
AUG 2001
BOTTLED AT CASK STRENGTH
THE BOTTLERS
FINE SINGLE ISLAY
SCOTCH MALT WHISKY
from Port Ellen Distillery
Cask No
1552
Cask Type - Refill Sherry Hogshead
Distilled and Bottled in Scotland
59.8% Alc by vol
70cl
DISTILLED FEB 1982
19
Years Old
AUG 2001
BOTTLED AT CASK STRENGTH
THE BOTTLERS
FINE SINGLE ISLAY
SCOTCH MALT WHISKY
from Port Ellen Distillery
Cask No
570
Cask Type - Refill Sherry Butt
Distilled and Bottled in Scotland
61.7% Alc by vol
70cl

AGED 12 YEARS
James MacArthur & Co Ltd
Fine Malt Selection
PORT ELLEN
SINGLE MALT
SCOTCH WHISKY
AGED
12 YEARS
DISTILLED & BOTTLED IN SCOTLAND
JAMES MACARTHUR & CO. LTD.
EDINBURGH
75cl e
62,7% vol
AGED 12 YEARS
James MacArthur & Co Ltd
Fine Malt Selection
PORT ELLEN
SINGLE MALT
SCOTCH WHISKY
AGED
12 YEARS
DISTILLED & BOTTLED IN SCOTLAND
JAMES MACARTHUR & CO. LTD.
EDINBURGH
BOTTLED FOR SCOMA GMBH
75cl e
59% vol

Established 1842
CADENHEAD'S
AUTHENTIC
COLLECTION
150th anniversary bottling
Single Malt Scotch Whisky
This whisky has been bottled from a selected individual cask in its natural state and shows the character of that cask. It has not been diluted with water. It has not been treated to change its colour and is free from all additives. It has not been subjected to any filtration that might remove natural constituents and spoil its flavour. It is the authentic product of its distillery.
Bottled by Wm. Cadenhead, 32 Union Street, Campbeltown, SCOTLAND
From
PORT ELLEN
Distillery
Distilled April 1981 and bottled July 1992
Matured in an oak cask
for 11 years
70cl
64.5%vol
Product of Scotland

A RARE VINTAGE BOTTLING
Estd 1988
FORTIS ET FIDELIS
HART BROTHERS
Finest Collection
SINGLE MALT SCOTCH WHISKY
AGED 19 YEARS
DISTILLED 1977 AT
PORT ELLEN DISTILLERY
ISLAY SCOTLAND
70cl
BOTTLED IN SCOTLAND BY HART BROTHERS (1988) LIMITED
43% vol
PRODUCT OF SCOTLAND
A RARE VINTAGE BOTTLING
Estd 1988
FORTIS ET FIDELIS
HART BROTHERS
Finest Collection
SINGLE MALT SCOTCH WHISKY
AGED 22 YEARS
DISTILLED 1975 AT
PORT ELLEN DISTILLERY
ISLAY SCOTLAND
70cl e
BOTTLED IN SCOTLAND BY HART BROTHERS (1988) LIMITED
43% vol
PRODUCT OF SCOTLAND
A RARE VINTAGE BOTTLING
Estd 1988
FORTIS ET FIDELIS
HART BROTHERS
Finest Collection
SINGLE MALT SCOTCH WHISKY
70cl e
AGED 23 YEARS
DISTILLED 1975 AT
PORT ELLEN DISTILLERY
ISLAY SCOTLAND
BOTTLED 1998 IN SCOTLAND BY HART BROTHERS (1988) LIMITED
PRODUCT OF SCOTLAND
A RARE VINTAGE BOTTLING
FORTIS ET FIDELIS
AGED 23 YEARS
DISTILLED APRIL 1975 AT
PORT ELLEN DISTILLERY
ISLAY SCOTLAND
BOTTLED JANUARY 1999 IN SCOTLAND BY HART BROTHERS LIMITED

HART BROTHERS
Single Malt Scotch Whisky
Distilled at the
PORT ELLEN
Distillery
AGED 19 YEARS
A RARE VINTAGE BOTTLING
Bottled in Scotland
Hart Brothers (1988) Ltd
70cl
A RARE VINTAGE BOTTLING
Estd 1988
FORTIS ET FIDELIS
HART
BROTHERS
Finest Collection
SINGLE MALT SCOTCH WHIS
AGED 19 YEARS
DISTILLED 1976 AT
PORT ELLEN DISTILLERY
ISLAY SCOTLAND
70cl
BOTTLED IN SCOTLAND BY
HART BROTHERS (1988) LIMITED

THE SCOTCH WHISKY SOCIETY
43.4
THE SCOTCH WHISKY SOCIETY
43.9
THE SCOTCH WHISKY SOCIETY
43.5
THE SCOTCH WHISKY SOCIETY
43.10
THE SCOTCH WHISKY SOCIETY
43.11
THE SCOTCH WHISKY SOCIETY
43.12
THE SCOTCH MALT WHISKY SOCIETY
THE VAULTS LEITH SCOTLAND
No. 43.13
THE SCOTCH MALT WHISKY SOCIETY
THE VAULTS LEITH SCOTLAND
No. 43.14

Old Malt Cask
Cask
DISTILLED AT
PORT ELLEN DISTILLERY
SINGLE MALT SCOTCH WHISKY
DISTILLED 1969 SEPTEMBER
BOTTLED 2001 MARCH
Aged 31 Years
NO CHILL FILTRATION. NO COLOURING
BOTTLED AT NATURAL CASK STRENGTH
Islay
THIS BOTTLE IS ONE
OF 41 BOTTLES
FILLED FROM CASK
Islay
DISTILLED, MATURED AND BOTTLED IN SCOTLAND
DOUGLAS LAING & CO LTD, GLASGOW G3 6EQ
PRODUCT OF SCOTLAND

The Old Malt Cask 50°
SINGLE MALT SCOTCH WHISKY
SINGLE Cask BOTTLING
DISTILLED AT
PORT ELLEN DISTILLERY
SINGLE MALT SCOTCH WHISKY
DISTILLED 1976 MARCH
BOTTLED 2001 APRIL
Aged 25 Years
NO CHILL FILTRATION. NO COLOURING
BOTTLED AT OUR PREFERRED STRENGTH OF 50% ALC/VOL
Islay · Islay
DISTILLED, MATURED AND BOTTLED IN SCOTLAND
DOUGLAS LAING & CO LTD. GLASGOW G3 6EQ
PRODUCT OF SCOTLAND
The McGibbon's
PROVENANCE
SPRING
DISTILLATION
Special - Selection
SINGLE MALT SCOTCH WHISKY
DISTILLED AT
PORT ELLEN DISTILLERY
ISLAY
Distilled - 1976 - Spring
Bottled - 2001 - Winter
OVER 24 YEARS
PRODUCT OF SCOTLAND
DISTILLED, MATURED & BOTTLED IN SCOTLAND
DOUGLAS MCGIBBON & CO. LTD., GLASGOW G3 6EQ
55.1% vol
~No colouring - not chill filtered~
Old Malt Cask 50°
SINGLE MALT SCOTCH WHISKY
A SINGLE Cask BOTTLING
DISTILLED AT
PORT ELLEN DISTILLERY
SINGLE MALT SCOTCH WHISKY
DISTILLED 1978 JANUARY
BOTTLED 2001 SEPTEMBER
Aged 23 Years
FINISHED IN SHERRY CASK-MINIMUM 6 MONTHS
NO CHILL FILTRATION. NO COLOURING
BOTTLED AT OUR PREFERRED STRENGTH OF 50% ALC/VOL
Islay · Islay
THIS BOTTLE IS ONE
OF 764 BOTTLES
FILLED FROM CASK
DISTILLED, MATURED AND BOTTLED IN SCOTLAND
DOUGLAS LAING & CO LTD. GLASGOW G3 6EQ
PRODUCT OF SCOTLAND

Sources

Chapter 1
1 Glenlochy.com-History
2 Andrew Jefford, Peat, Smoke and Spirit: The Story of Islay and its Whiskies, Headline Book Publishing, 2004 p. 145-146
3 Ibid p. 145
4 Neil Wilson, Scotch and Water, Lochar Publishing, 1985 p. 61
5 John Ramsay p. 15 see also Neil Wilson p. 62
6 Neil Wilson, p. 63
7 Craig p. 100
8 Andrew Jefford p. 140
9 Neil Wilson p. 64
10 John R. Hume & Michael S. Moss The Making of Scotch whisky, Canongate, ed. 2000 p. 112
11 Neil Wilson p. 52
12 Margaret Storrie, p. 168
13 David H Caldwell., Islay: The Land of the Lordship Birlinn Ltd 2008 p. 117
14 John R. Hume & Michael S. Moss p. 112
15 Alfred Barnad, p.
16 David H Caldwell, p. 263
17 Neil Wilson p. 65
18 Townsend Brian, Scotch missed: Lost distilleries of Scotland, Angel's share, 3rd Edition, 2004 p. 33
19 Neil Wilson p. 65
20 Ibid p. 65
21 Ibid p. 47
22 Ibid p. 35
23 Ibid p. 56
24 Ibid p. 66
25 Ibid p. 66
26 John A. Thomson, Port Ellen, Distillery and Maltings, Diageo, 2007 p.6

Chapter 2
27 Margaret Storrie p. 213
28 John A. Thomson p. 6
29 Ulf Buxrud, Rare Malts, Facts, Figures and Taste, Quiller Press, 2006 p.147
30 Ibid p. 143
31 Ibid p. 143
32 Ibid p. 143, see also John A. Thomson p. 7
33 John A. Thomson p. 7-8
34 Andrew Jefford p. 371
35 Gavin D. Smith, Wort, warms and washbacks, p. 29
36 Diageo Archive
37 Diageo Archive
38 Neil Wilson p. 66; Gawin D. Smith 2013 Stillhouse Storries p. 49
39 Grant Carmichael E-Mail 2002
40 Andrew Jefford p. 371
41 Ibid p. 371
42 Ibid p. 371
43 Ulf Buxrud, p. 144
44 Serge Valentin, Malt Maniacs Issue 17, Internet, France 31.01.2006

Chapter 3
45 Loch Fyne Whisky Interview with Professor Ronnie Martin O. B. E. from SWR Edition 5, Spring 1996
46 Andrew Jefford p. 281
47 Whisky Magazine No. 66, Ask the expert
48 Neil Wilson p. 48
49 Andrew Jefford p. 370-371

Chapter 4
50 Neil Wilson p. 67
51 Ingvar Ronde Malt Whisky Yearbook 2011
52 THE ILEACH Vol. 30 No.14 in 17 May 2003 p.2

Chapter 5

53 Buxton Ian, Glenglassaugh, Angel's share 2010 p.45
54 Interview of the Brands & Cigar Consultants Jens Tausch with Arthur Winning
55 cf. E-mail, Diageo Archive, Nov.2012
56 E-Mail Grant Carmichael 2002
57 Ingvar Ronde, Malt Whisky Yearbook 2010, p.13
58 October 2013 Dr. Morgan American whiskycast
59 The Guardian, 26 Oct. 2013
60 E-mail from (Laing) December 2012
61 E-mail from Fred Laing, February 2012
62 Schobert Walther, Malt Whisky Guide, p.174

Photographs

Cover: Port Ellen Distillery 1920, Museum of Islay Life
Port Ellen Double Kiln, H. Dreyer
Page 6/7 Port Ellen Workforce 1906 Museum of Islay Life
Page 8/9Port Ellen Distillery 1920, Museum of Islay Life
Page 10 Port Ellen Cask 1906, Museum of Islay Life
Page 15 Port Ellen bottle, Lothar Langer
Page 16 Port Ellen bottle, Lothar Langer
Page 17 Port Ellen Port Ellen Workforce 1895, Museum of Islay Life
Page 18 Port Ellen Workforce 1906, Museum of Islay Life
Page 20 Port Ellen Distillery from sea 1920, Museum of Islay Life
Page 21 Port Ellen Distillery 1935, Diageo Archive
Page 22 Port Ellen Maltings, M. Bohnsack
Port Ellen Pibroch list, 1968, Port Ellen Maltings
Port Ellen Manager, reopening April 1967, whiskyfun.com
Page 23 Port Ellen First Cask, M.Bohnsack
Port Ellen distillery in the sixties, Diageo Archive
Page 24 Port Ellen stills leaving Abercrombie, Diageo Archive
Page 25 Port Ellen stills installation, Diageo Archive
Page 26 Port Ellen stillhouse, Diageo Archive
Page 28 Port Ellen malting floors, Diageo Archive
Page 29 Port Ellen Spirit Safe, Diageo Archive
Page 30 Port Ellen stillhouse, Diageo Archive
Page 31 Port Ellen casks from 1967, Diageo Archive
Page 32/33 Port Ellen stillhouse, Diageo Archive
Page 34/35 Port Ellen stillhouse-spirit condenser 1969, Museum of Islay Life
Page 36 Port Ellen washbacks, Port Ellen Maltings
Page 38 Old guns Blend, Sukhinder Singh
Page 39 Port Ellen distillery entrance 1989, Markus from Schwerin
SMD warehouse stamp, 1989, Markus from Schwerin
Page 40/41 Port Ellen stillhouse, spirit safe 1989, Markus from Schwerin
Page 42 Port Ellen Stillhouse 1996, Prof. W. Schobert
Page 43 Port Ellen stillhouse, 1998 B. Ring
Port Ellen tunroom, 1998, B. Ring
Page 44 Evacator, 2003, H. Dreyer
Page 45 Still foundations, 2003, H. Dreyer
Page 46 Port Ellen entrance, 2003 H. Dreyer
Port Ellen buildings, 2003, H. Dreyer
Page 47 Port Ellen Double kiln, 2003, H. Dreyer
Port Ellen red pagoda, 2003, H. Dreyer
Page 48 Port Ellen steering unit for the mash-tun, Port Ellen mash tun, Port Ellen red pagoda, Port Ellen yellow tunroom door, Port Ellen rest of fromer tunroom, Port Ellen former stillhouse and tunroom, all pictures taken by H. Dreyer

Page 49 Port Ellen warehouses from the sea, Heinz Fesl; Port Ellen warehouses from the shore, W. Hobler; Port Ellen distillery from the sea, 2003, T. Döpke; Port Ellen distillery II from the sea, 2003, T. Döpke
Page 50 Port Ellen warehouses from the shore, M. Bohnsack
Page 51 Port Ellen first cask, cask end, 2013, M. Bohnsack
Port Ellen maltings, 2014, H. Dreyer
Port Ellen double kiln, 2014, H. Dreyer
Port Ellen last cask, 2013, M. Bohnsack
Port Ellen double kiln from the mainland, 2014, H. Dreyer,
Port Ellen double kiln, 2014, H. Dreyer
Page 52 Port Ellen warehouse complex, 2014, all pictures taken by H. Dreyer
Page 55 Port Ellen first cask, cask end, 2013, M. Bohnsack
Page 56 Port Ellen cask 1979, warehouse G&M-Elgin, M. Prinz
Port Ellen cask 1979, H. Dreyer
Page 57 Port Ellen cask 1979, R. Ellinghaus
Bottling Label The Ultimate, H. Dreyer
Page 58 Port Ellen cask 1981, H. Dreyer
Page 59 Port Ellen cask 1982, Ian MacLeod
Port Ellen cask 1983, Duncan Taylor

Photography of the Port Ellen bottles copyright H. Dreyer with the exception of the following images:
Page 65 Port Ellen Queens decanter, supplied by Sukhinder Singh
Page 74 Port Ellen bottling Feis Ilse 2008, supplied by Sukhinder Singh
Page 90 Port Ellen bottlings of the Scotch Malt Whisky Society supplied by Rheinhard Ellinghaus

Bibliography

Archives:
Diageo Archive
Museum of Islay

Published Books

Barnard Alfred, The Whisky Distilleries of the United Kingdom, Year 2000 Reprint, Rascheedition
Buxton Ian, Glenglassaugh, Angel's share 2010
Buxton Ian, The Enduring Legacy of Dewars: A Company History, Angel's share, 1st Edition, 2010
Buxrud Ulf, Rare Malts, Facts, Figures and Taste, Quiller Press, 2006
Caldwell David H., Islay: The Land of the Lordship Birlinn Ltd (October 2008)
Craig H. Charles, Scotch Whisky Industry Record: An Industry History and Reference Book 1994
Hume John R. & Moss Michael S, The Making of Scotch whisky, Canongate, ed. 2000.
Jefford Andrew, Peat, Smoke and Spirit: The Story of Islay and its Whiskies, Headline Book Publishing, 2004
Offringa Hans and van Gils Marcel, The Legend of Laphroaig, Still publishing, 2007
Paterson Richard & Gavin Smith Goodness nose, Angel's share, 2008
Ronde Ingvar, Malt Whisky Yearbook 2010, 5th Edition, MagDig Media Ltd, 2009
Ronde Ingvar, Malt Whisky Yearbook 2012, 7th Edition, MagDig Media Ltd, 2011
Schobert Walther, Malt Whisky Guide, Führer zu den Quellen, 2012 (german)
Smith Gavin D. & Wallace Graeme, Ardbeg: A peaty Provenance, GW Publishing, 2008

Smith Gavin D. Stillhouse Storries, Tunroom tales, Neil Wilson Publishing 2013
Spiller Brian, Port Ellen Distillery and Maltings, The Distillers Company Limited 1981
Thomson John A., Port Ellen, Distillery and Maltings, Diageo, 2007
Townsend Brian, Scotch missed: Lost distilleries of Scotland, Angel's share, 3rd Edition, 2004
Townsend Brian, Scotch missed: Lost distilleries of Scotland, Angel's share, 4st Edition, 2015
Wilson Neil, Scotch and Water, Lochar Publishing, 1985

Whisky Magazines:

LFW Interview with Professor Ronnie Martin O. B. E. from SWR Edition 5, Spring 1996
LFW Interview with Dr, Alan Rutherford from SWR Edition 2, Autumn 1994
LFW Interview with Turnbull Hutton Operations Director of Distillation and Spirit Supply Spring 2001
Schobert Walther, Whisky watch Issue No.21 August 2003 (german)
The Society Newsletter, SMWS Issue 67, Spring 2001 Port Ellen Maltings S.4-5

Newspapers

The Guardian, 26 Oct. 2013

Internet

Interview of the Brands & Cigar Consultants Jens Tausch with the owner and founder of James MacArthur, Artur Winning
Submitted 31/01/2006 by www.maltmaniacs.org
Serge Valentin, France Malt-Maniacs Issue 17
Whisky Cast, Episode 447, October 12, 2013

Acknowledgements

During my studies for this book I was assisted by many people. I would like to thank the following for contributing to this book:
Dr. Matthias Bohnsack, Patrick Brossard, Stefan Bügler, Grant Carmichael, Frank Danielzik, Dr. Thomas Döpke, Dr. Reinhard Ellinghaus, Heinz Fesl, John Glass, IanMacleod Distillers Ltd, Lothar Langer, Whiskyraritäten, Fred Laing, Stewart Laing, Dr. Jürgen Lemme, Maggie Miller Scotch Single Malt Circle, Jenni Minto and Christine from the Museum of Islay Life, Christine McCafferty from Diageo Archive, Dr. Mario Prinz, Bärbel & Ludwig Reifferscheid, Kay Riddoch, Duncan Taylor Scotch Whisky Limited, Dr. Benno Ring, Dirk Siemer, Sukhinder Singh, The WhiskyExchange, Prof. Walther Schobert, Serge Valentin, Bernd Wolf
My special thanks go to my wife Annette Dreyer for the layout and digital image processing and my friend P. Nath for translating many parts from German to English.

Whoever I forgot, please accept my sincere apologies and let me know, so that I can include the names in the next print.

Final remark in October 2015
It was impossible -because of unknown copyright ownership - to publish all photographs. I am always interested in photographs and stories from the time after the reopening of Port Ellen distillery in 1966/1967.
Please contact me at LowRobertson63@yahoo.de

Holger Dreyer, MA